Global Marketing for the Digital Age

Global Marketing for the Digital Age

Globalize Your Business with Digital and Online Technology

BILL BISHOP

HarperBusiness
HarperCollins*PublishersLtd*

http://www.harpercollins.com/canada

First edition

The following terms are trademarks of Bishop Information Group Inc.: Marketing
Technopia™, Technopia™, The Global Digital Marketing Model™, The Global
Digital Marketing Index™, The Strategic Digital Marketing Model™, Your Global
Digital Vision™, Your Global Digital Market™, The New Digital World Order™.

Canadian Cataloguing in Publication Data

Bishop, Bill, 1957-
Global marketing for the digital age : globalize your business
with digital and online technology

"A HarperBusiness book"
ISBN 0-00-255740-1

1. Marketing - Data processing.   2. Database marketing.   3. Teleshopping.
4. Internet marketing.   5. Marketing - Technological innovations.   I. Title.

HF 5415.1265.B57 1996   658.8'00285   C96-930733-0

96 97 98 99 WEB 10 9 8 7 6 5 4 3 2 1

Printed and bound in Canada

To Ginny

My global gal

CONTENTS

SECTION FOUR

ACKNOWLEDGMENTS

When you think about someone who has written a book, you marvel at the dedication, determination, and creativity of the author. But you rarely consider the plight of the poor souls who nurture the author, those loved ones and coworkers who endure the temper tantrums, the despair, the manic intensity, and the general instability of said writer. In my case, there is a legion of supporters who deserve mention. Let me begin with Ginny, my life partner and soul mate. She has tirelessly encouraged and coddled me throughout the gestation of this book, and my previous one. For her patience and undying loyalty, I dedicate this book to her.

In the second tier of those who have tirelessly kept the faith, my business partner Curtis Verstraete helped keep my wild fancies in check and was instrumental in getting the book in shipshape. My mother Priscilla, an Internet surf-bunny in her eighth decade, gets a hearty applause for keeping the office running smoothly while I attended to the book. Lynne Shuttleworth, my journalist colleague, helped edit and proofread this tome. Don Loney, my editor at HarperCollins, and copy editor Jane Lind, always maintained their professional demeanor. And finally, I want to thank my son Douglas, who has given me hope for the future and has never complained while I worked away on my book.

In the third row, the group grows larger. They are my clients, investors, workshop participants, suppliers, and business partners, who deserve an award for helping transform my company, BIG Inc., into one of North America's leading digital marketing companies. In no particular order, they are Dr. Doug Biggar, John Narvali, Malcolm Silver, Michael Caron, Normand Mailhot, Peter Creaghan, Sara Creaghan, Steve Sills, Terry Whelpton, Cindy Goldrick, Diana Bishop, Judith Tropianskaia, Steve Barrett, Sholan Zaio, Susan Johnson, Tim Tevlin, Mary Birch, Jean-Pierre Lacroix, Karim Munjee, Danny Shay, Dan Sullivan, Linda Lundstrom, Michael Shanahan, Jennifer Whelpton, Sandra Matheson, Neil Erickson, Susan Thomas, Judy Biggar, Patrick Mann, David Sambrook, Ian Percy, Pat Bradley, John Beauchamp, Owen Smith, Peter Shenstone, Richard Hagle, Ron Fisher, Lyndell Hastings, Peter Zarry, Natasha Murray, Paul Lermitte, Gerald I. Kalish, Steve Lichty, Sabine Steinbrecher, Grant Humes, Shannon Smith, Jim Clemmer, and Dr. Mohammad Alatar.

I would also be remiss if I didn't acknowledge the fine work done by my digital and online assistants. I want to thank my numerous Macintosh computers, whom I will defend forever against the PC onslaught. I want to thank my word processing program, Microsoft Works, and my FirstClass BBS system for allowing everyone involved in this project to work together efficiently. I owe a "thank you" to our database program, Claris Filemaker Pro, which was used to compile the Global Digital Marketing Index.

To everyone listed above, and anyone else whose assistance I've failed to acknowledge, thank you. I hope you are looking forward to helping me with my next book, and the one after that, and the one after that ...

PREFACE

THE SECOND AGE OF GLOBAL EXPLORATION

Before the 15th century, few Europeans had ventured purposefully beyond the Pillars of Hercules, a narrow strait linking the Mediterranean to the vast watery expanse now known as the Atlantic Ocean. What lay beyond the British Isles was a matter of speculation. The earth was thought to be flat. Venture too far, and you were sure to drop off into some kind of void. So keeping within the familiar confines of the Mediterranean Sea seemed the sensible thing to do. It was not until Christopher Columbus returned to Spain to report on his voyage to America, and Vasco da Gama sailed around the Horn of Africa to India, that the European world came to appreciate the true size and nature of our magnificent planet. This period of discovery was the First Age of Global Exploration.

While writing this book about global marketing, this thought struck me: we have entered the Second Age of Global Exploration. Using e-mail, the World Wide Web, global telecommunications, fax machines, cellular telephones, satellites, and other digital wonders, the explorers of our time are venturing into strange and wonderful new worlds. Like the great explorers—Columbus, Magellan, Balboa, Cabot, Cartier, and Drake—today's digital marketers are using the technology of their time to expand their markets, find new customers, and reap financial rewards.

When I compare these two epochs, another idea becomes apparent: No matter what age you live in, you need courage to explore the world beyond your horizon. When seafaring explorers left port for distant lands, bravery was their most vital asset. Can you imagine setting out across the Atlantic Ocean in a small, wooden ship without charts, refrigeration, or communications equipment? Can you picture landing on an unknown Pacific island to be met by frightened—and frightening—natives? Can you see yourself entering the frigid waters of Hudson Bay with the mistaken notion you were sailing the Northwest Passage to the Far East? I can't. But these explorers of yesteryear—who forged the way for us—had a brand of courage we can only imagine.

The global marketers of our digital age also need their own brand of courage. It takes bravery to reach across a national, cultural, or linguistic boundary, even if it's only over the telephone or through an e-mail message. It takes courage to commit yourself and your company to a business venture in other countries. You must deal with different cultures and new ways of doing business. You must introduce your products and services to people who have never heard of you before. You also may be required to speak another language or behave in a way that is foreign to you. All of this, and more, takes courage.

Luckily, there are two differences between global marketing in the digital age and exploration in the 15th century. First, unlike Columbus and Magellan, you have what I hope will be a reliable chart to lead the way: this book. Using the ideas and structure presented here, you don't have to worry about falling off the face of the earth. Second, using the Internet and other digital wonders, you don't need to leave your office to begin your global exploration. With a few clicks of your mouse, you can sail around the world in a matter of seconds. You don't have to worry about getting scurvy or being stuck in the doldrums. I hope you enjoy and benefit from reading *Global Marketing for the Digital Age*.

Bill Bishop
March 1998

INTRODUCING
GLOBAL DIGITAL MARKETING

CHAPTER 1

YOUR GLOBAL ODYSSEY

Tell me, Muse, the story of that resourceful man who was driven to wander far and wide after he had sacked the holy citadel of Troy. He saw the cities of many people and he learnt their ways. He suffered great anguish on the high seas in his struggles to preserve his life and bring his comrades home.

The Odyssey
Homer

In the eighth century B.C., when Homer wrote *The Odyssey*, the Greeks believed the Mediterranean was the center of the universe. Anywhere a few hundred miles from Greece was thought to be the outer reaches of the cosmos, and the people who lived on the fringes were viewed as strange. In the first chapter of *The Odyssey*, for example, the god Poseidon visits the "distant" Ethiopians, "in the most remote part of the world."

Obviously, a lot has changed since Odysseus made his peripatetic voyage home to Ithaca from Troy. Today, the same trip takes less than an hour by plane. To visit the distant Ethiopians today, Poseidon could travel from Athens to Addis Ababa in about four hours. Better still, he wouldn't need to fly. Greeks can communicate with Ethiopians at the speed of light, using digital and online tools such as the telephone, fax machines, video-conferencing, e-mail, and the World Wide Web.

But in spite of our fabulous technology, some things haven't changed in the past 28 centuries. Although we have become a global village in some ways, and tourism has become a huge industry, most of us still prefer to stay close to our own backyard. We still feel safer on our home turf, surrounded by familiar people, places, and customs.

When it comes to business, however, home isn't what it used to be. Until recently, it was possible to prosper in your local market. In a relatively simple economy, and with little competition from outside, you could make a living selling your wares to customers in your own community. In general, marketing your products and services in other countries was not practical. These markets were too far away, and it was very expensive to visit them in person, to look for new customers. And if you did get foreign customers, it was very difficult to deal with them on a regular basis. You had to pay high rates for long-distance calls and had to deal with complicated tariffs and regulations. For these reasons, and many more, global marketing was the domain of only the largest and most powerful corporations.

Today, however, every business person can, and must, adopt a global marketing perspective. With the rapid growth of digital and online technology around the world, it's not only possible for every business to operate on a global scale, it's essential, for a number of reasons.

Competitive Local Markets. As I said, your local market has become crowded with products and services. Your competitors now come from the four corners of the globe. Because they reach the much larger, worldwide market, your global-savvy competition is able to achieve better economies of scale. (This means they can produce larger volumes of a product or service, which brings down the total cost per unit.) They also often have access to much cheaper labor. These factors help your competitors deliver products and services that are inexpensive and of comparable or higher quality.

The Globalization of Trade. Around the world, barriers to trade—such as tariffs, import quotas, and regulatory restrictions—are being dismantled. Through trade agreements and trading blocs such as GATT, NAFTA, and the European Union, the major economies of the world have lowered as many trade barriers as possible. They see open trade as the best way to foster strong economic growth in their respective countries. This trend away from protectionism to more open worldwide trade conditions means there are fewer and fewer national boundaries to hide behind.

The Cosmopolitan Consumer. In today's global economy, consumers have become cosmopolitan in their buying habits. They have lost almost all loyalty to local producers. They don't care if a product or service is produced in the United States, Taiwan, or India. They want the best quality, for the best price, period. This trend is best illustrated by cross-border shopping and Internet shopping. Consumers who wish to take advantage of exchange-rate disparities flock, in person or electronically, to a neighboring country where prices are lower. Because of this lack of loyalty, you can no longer rely on your local customers to buy at home first.

The Victory of the Specialist. In today's complex worldwide economy, the specialist has triumphed over the generalist. A company that focuses on a specific product or service will win out over a business that tries to be all things to all people. The specialist who produces one thing can achieve the economies of scale needed to take advantage of a global economy that offers a large, viable market for specialty products and services. (See below The Case of the Global Bread Stick.)

The Falling Cost of Global Business. In this book we examine closely how digital and online technology is driving down the cost of operating a business on a global scale. Long-distance telephone rates are falling worldwide and will continue to fall because of deregulation and other competitive factors. Low-cost communication tools—

such as e-mail, private online networks, and the World Wide Web— are rapidly being adopted in all the major countries. (See the Global Digital Marketing Index.) This combination of lower telephone rates and the global proliferation of low-cost communication tools makes running a global marketing program much easier and less expensive.

All of these factors, and many others, make it necessary for you to consider expanding your market beyond your borders. Whether you are the marketing director of a major corporation or the owner of a home business, you must set your sights on distant horizons if you wish to prosper. Your local market may no longer be big enough to sustain you. You have to go global! As an example, let's examine a case study of a hypothetical company that has grown from a local concern to a more profitable global business.

THE CASE OF THE GLOBAL BREAD STICK

When Anthony Rex started his restaurant on the Lower East Side in Manhattan, no one suspected he would one day become the world's bread stick mogul. After all, Tony's ambitions were modest. His goal was to run the best Italian bistro in the neighborhood, and within a few years, he was doing a booming business. Although most people loved his pasta and pizza, everyone raved about his bread sticks made from a recipe handed down through his family for generations. There was something about the bread sticks people couldn't get enough of, and Tony started selling them in packages for his patrons to take home. In no time, Tony's bread sticks became the toast of Manhattan. But the bread sticks got so popular that Tony was spending all his time making them, and the restaurant began to suffer.

Tony was caught between a bread stick and a hard place. Should he go back and focus on the restaurant or make a go of it selling bread sticks? Tony thought the bread sticks could be much more popular than the restaurant, but he realized his local market, even a city the size of New York, was not large enough to sustain a bread stick empire. Tony decided that his destiny lay in these cigar-shaped appetizers, and he began in earnest to develop his global marketing program.

He started by developing a vision for the future of his business. Looking ahead, Tony envisioned selling his T-Rex Bread Stick line to restaurants and individuals around the world. He set a goal of selling $5 million worth of bread sticks annually by the end of the third year. He also envisioned running his entire global operation using low-cost digital and online technology.

Tony's second step was to research the global market. By referring to the countries rated in the Global Digital Marketing Index (see Chapter 11), Tony chose 10 countries that rated high on the Index because of their economic power, political stability, openness to trade, and advanced digital and online capabilities. Using his Internet connection, Tony accessed the Web sites listed in the Index to look for potential trading partners within each country. Within a few hours of surfing the Net, Tony discovered a number of restaurant chains, food importers, and other entrepreneurs who, he thought, would be interested in being his partner in each target country. Tony entered these prospects into his customer database, bookmarked their sites on his browser, and saved their e-mail addresses.

In tandem with this research, he developed a Web site called Bread Stick World, the first Internet site solely dedicated to the subject of bread sticks. The site featured everything you ever wanted to know about bread sticks, along with bread stick chat rooms, bread stick trivia, and links to bread-stick-related sites around the world. Of course, the site also featured glorious photos of Tony's bread sticks, celebrity testimonials, and even a sound clip of T-Rex Bread Sticks being enjoyed by the G8 leaders at a summit luncheon.

With everything in place, Tony began sending out e-mail messages to his prospects, inviting them to visit Bread Stick World and read about the popularity of his bread sticks. Within days, a number of the prospects came to the site and filled out an extensive survey in exchange for a free shipment of bread sticks. Within a few months, Tony's global digital marketing program began to pay off handsomely. Agents from around the world, whom Tony had never met except through e-mail, loved the bread sticks and started ordering large shipments through the World Wide Web. (Tony also set up a global toll-free number for prospects to call his office from any country in the world at no charge.) The bread sticks were baked to order and shipped overnight by air in special stay-fresh containers to restaurants and specialty grocery stores.

After three years, Tony had achieved his sales goal and was running a bread stick manufacturing facility in New Jersey just across the river from Manhattan. T-Rex Bread Sticks were on their way to becoming the most popular brand in the world. Using digital and online technology, he had developed excellent relationships with dozens of high-quality bread stick agents. In addition, Bread Stick World became one of the top sites on the Internet and fostered a number of spin-off products including *Bread Stick Life*, a magazine celebrating bread stick culture, the Bread Stick Video Series, and the Bread Stick Lover's Retreat in the British Virgin Islands.

As you can see, Tony's success resulted from his global vision. If he had focused only on Manhattan, he would not have found enough customers to develop a large-scale business. He would have had to keep running the restaurant, which would have kept him from exploiting his specialty, his ancestors' bread sticks. As well, he took advantage of digital and online technology to reach out and communicate with potential customers. If he had been forced to visit each of his target countries in person, he would not have been able to afford it. With e-mail and the World Wide Web, he was able to find prospects using only the computer in *his* office. And his prospects learned about the T-Rex Bread Sticks without leaving *their* office. And finally, Tony served his new clients effectively by using online ordering and overnight worldwide shipping.

Of course, not all of us can become bread stick tycoons, but I believe every business person can develop a specialty and has the potential and the ability to operate on a global scale. Because of this belief, I wrote this book to:

- show you how to use digital and online technology to reach a global market;
- provide you with a structure for developing a global marketing program; and
- offer you lots of global marketing ideas that you can use for your business.

THE SCOPE OF THIS BOOK

Global Marketing for the Digital Age takes over where my previous book, *Strategic Marketing for the Digital Age*, leaves off. Like its predecessor, this book is divided into sections and is presented in a step-by-step format. If you read each chapter in sequence, and follow the suggested steps in the order they are given, you can begin to develop your global marketing program while reading this book. The action-bias is important because strategic planning is most effective when accompanied by direct and immediate action. Here is a summary of the chapters to come.

Chapter 2: Strategic Digital Marketing. Effective global digital marketing depends on the appropriate use of digital and online technology. In this chapter, I explain how digital marketing is different from mass marketing, and I present a review of the Strategic Digital Marketing Model, which was first presented in *Strategic Marketing for the Digital Age*. As well, I explain the dangers of Marketing Technopia, the name I've given to a debilitating disease which afflicts people and companies that become obsessed with technology.

Chapter 3: The Eight Global Marketing Imperatives. If you want to go global, the way you do business will have to change. This chapter looks at changes you must make before you can succeed at global marketing.

Chapter 4: The Global Digital Marketing Model. Before you develop your global marketing program, you need an overall conceptual framework to guide you. Like the Strategic Digital Marketing Model, this model is based on updated marketing concepts, which account for the changes affecting the global and digital marketing environments.

SECTION TWO: Your Global Digital Marketing Program. This section provides global digital marketing ideas and background information, and a step-by-step method for developing your global digital marketing program.

Chapter 5: Your Global Digital Vision. To succeed at global marketing, you must create a vision for your company in the global marketplace. Without this vision, and clearly defined business objectives, your marketing efforts will lack focus and effectiveness. With a vision, your efforts will be much more strategic and much more effective in helping you achieve your business goals. This chapter explains why a global vision is important and provides 10 model structures for operating a global business.

Chapter 6: Your Global Digital Market. A global digital marketing program must be designed to reach the right kind of prospects in the right countries. This chapter explains how to determine your target markets, how to segment them into distinct groups, how to set up a customer database, and how to choose the most appropriate countries for your program.

Chapter 7: Your Global Digital Marketing Promotion. To attract the attention of your prospects in the global marketplace, you need to use digital and online technology in a strategic fashion. This chapter looks at dozens of different global promotional concepts and provides numerous examples of how you can put these concepts together to create a comprehensive global digital marketing program.

Chapter 8: Global Digital Technology. The opportunities for global marketing have been greatly enhanced by the worldwide development of digital and online technology. To succeed, you must choose the tools that match your vision, target market, and global marketing strategies. This chapter examines the global marketing applications of databases, global telecommunications, interactive voice response (IVR), call centers, e-mail, the World Wide Web, private online networks, fax, fax-on-demand, smart cards, and PUSH technology.

Chapter 9: Integrated Global Digital Marketing. This chapter presents five examples of fully integrated global digital marketing programs.

SECTION THREE: The Global Digital Marketing Environment. This section features an overview of global marketing conditions, including a detailed look at the major trading countries around the world.

Chapter 10: The New Digital World Order. As digital and online technology becomes more prevalent around the world, the presence of this technology will have a profound effect on the fortunes of all national economies. This chapter examines the global impact of digital technology and presents the case that only free, open, and democratic societies can prosper in the digital age.

Chapter 11: The Global Digital Marketing Index. In the world today, there are about 50 prospective countries for a global digital marketer. This chapter looks at all 50 and rates them according to the economic, political, and technological conditions that will affect the growth of their digital economy. In addition, key, trade-related Web sites are listed for each country, along with a detailed analysis of each nation's potential as a global digital partner.

SECTION FOUR: Appendixes. The first appendix, Resources, provides a description and Web site addresses for numerous organizations that can help you with your global marketing program. The following appendixes, a glossary of terms and a list of suggested readings, give you quick access to the information you'll need to understand and to delve more deeply into the digital marketing world.

GLOBAL DIGITAL MARKETING ONLINE

In this book, I have included ideas, relevant information, and a step-by-step structure to help you get started at global digital marketing. But the subject is huge—as big as the whole world—and no book can possibly cover the complete topic in one volume. In addition, as time marches on, new information and data are made available. That's why I created Global Digital Marketing Online. While reading this book, visit this site (**www.biginc.com**) to get updated statistics on each country rated in the Global Digital Marketing Index, links to trade-related sites in each country, and a forum for exchanging ideas and information with other global marketers.

So if you're ready, let's begin your global odyssey.

CHAPTER 2

STRATEGIC DIGITAL MARKETING

*Mention must be made of the most amazing of all voyages—
that of Necho with Phoenician sailers around Africa, the only
circumnavigation of that continent known to have occurred
before that of Vasco da Gama.*

Ancient Greek Mariners
Walter Woodburn Hyde

Like Necho's journey before da Gama, *Strategic Marketing for the Digital Age,* my previous book, charted a lot of territory to be covered in this chapter, although we're now looking at a global context. I explained how the digital marketing environment is fundamentally different from the traditional, mass-marketing environment that preceded it. Understanding the distinction between the two eras is important because you can't apply outmoded concepts in today's digital marketplace. Following principles from the bygone days of mass-media marketing is a recipe for complete disaster.

To help you plan an effective digital marketing program, the previous book presents the Strategic Digital Marketing Model, a step-by-step process you can use to develop your digital strategy. I have worked with, and heard from, hundreds of companies and individuals who have used this model successfully. So before you embark on the larger task of global marketing, it's useful to review these key points from the model.

THE DIGITAL MARKETING ENVIRONMENT

More and more consumers around the world use digital and online communications—such as the World Wide Web, interactive voice response (IVR), smart cards, fax-on-demand, and global 1-800 numbers—to do banking, find books, buy and sell cars, reserve airline tickets, and for a million other reasons. At the same time, marketers have discovered their customers and prospects do, in fact, use this technology for commercial purposes. With this realization, many business people who were initially skeptical are now rushing headlong into digital marketing without first thinking through their strategy. In addition, they don't understand how digital marketing (fueled by the microchip) is different from mass marketing (driven by broadcast television and radio, newspapers, billboard advertising, direct mail, telemarketing, and other mass communications). They need to understand that the digital marketing environment is:

- **Nonintrusive**: Unlike mass-marketing promotions such as television commercials or highway billboards, which catch your attention intrusively, digital marketing promotions, such as Web sites or private online networks (BBS), are essentially nonintrusive. For example, a television commercial is intrusive. While you are watching a football game, a beer commercial comes on. Before you can click with your remote to another channel, you have been exposed to the advertising message. However, digital promotions are generally not as intrusive. For example, unless people have a good reason to access your Web site or BBS, they will never see it or use it. For this reason, you must attract their attention by providing something valuable, such as useful, hard-to-get information or a value-added service that helps them do something easier, faster, or more economically. As such, you can't create a Web page and expect everyone on the Internet to flock to it. In fact, the sad truth is that a Web site is akin to a billboard tucked away on an obscure country road. Unless people know it exists and have a reason to go there, they are never going to see it.

- **Mercurial**: As the pace of technological change accelerates, the digital marketing environment will continue to evolve. Digital and online technology will become more widespread, and new information tools will be introduced. In their wake, the marketing environment will naturally adapt and mutate in response. That's why it's essential for you to keep learning about digital marketing and why it's important that your strategy be independent of, rather than dependent on, any specific technology.

- **Process oriented**: Mass marketing is *project* oriented. In contrast, digital marketing is *process* oriented. In the mass-marketing environment, you spend time developing a brochure, an advertising campaign, a direct-mail program, or a newsletter. Each of these programs is an isolated activity requiring a specific amount of time and money. In the digital age, marketing is more fluid and ongoing. You need to have people and resources to work on your digital marketing program on a continuous basis. For example, you need to update your Web site or fax-on-demand system regularly. You need to respond to e-mail enquiries as they are received. You need to take incoming customer calls 24 hours a day. In other words, digital marketing is always happening, and you need to be on call at all times. If not, your customers may take their business elsewhere. For example, I know of one company that put an e-mail address on a brochure and distributed thousands of copies around the world. For nine months no one bothered to look in the e-mail box, and when they did, there were thousands of messages in it. Some of the people wrote, "Hello, are you there? Is anyone there?" Fortunately, the company now has someone who checks the e-mail box every day and directs messages to the appropriate people for immediate response. So keep in mind that digital marketing is a fluid, ongoing process.

- **Results oriented**: Digital marketing is much more results oriented than mass marketing. By its very nature, digital technology allows you to track the bottom-line results you achieve from your marketing promotions. For example, using a private online network, you can receive an e-mail message the moment someone opens one of the documents on your system. Every time someone buys something on your Web site, you receive a message indicating who made the purchase, what they bought, how much they bought, and how much they have spent over a particular period of time. Using a database, you can capture the names of prospects who visit your site and keep track of how many actually buy something from you at a future date, either online or at one of your stores. Each of these examples illustrates how results-oriented data can be gleaned using digital technology. That's why I advise my clients to ignore "hits" as a way to measure the impact of their Web site. Hits are the equivalent of "gross rating points," "impressions," or other measurement terms used for mass marketing. Measurement methods such as "hits" only give you a general indication of the overall impact of your promotion. In the digital marketing environment, you can, and should, be much more results oriented. Ask yourself or your suppliers: "How many sales did we make because of our Web site? How many new leads did we get?" Don't settle for vague answers. Demand specific results.

- **Spatial, not linear**: In mass marketing, each step in the process happens in a linear fashion. Market research is followed by product development, which is followed by promotion, which is followed by customer service. Each step is completely separate from the one preceding it and the one that follows. In the digital marketing environment, all of the steps happen simultaneously. Market research is conducted by your customer service representatives when they are talking to your customers about a warranty issue. New products are developed as you receive feedback from your customers on your Web site. Promotions are created to generate demand for products that haven't been developed yet. In the digital marketing environment, all of these activities happen simultaneously and have an impact on each other. An understanding of the spatial nature of digital marketing is essential to success.

- **Not just about the World Wide Web**: When I refer to digital marketing, I'm not talking about Internet marketing or Web marketing. I believe marketers who focus solely on the Internet are missing a much bigger picture. Digital marketing involves scores of digital and online tools such as databases, e-mail, the telephone, prepaid calling cards, private online networks, proprietary software, electronic forms, CD-ROM/DVD, bar codes, PUSH technology, pagers, cellular telephones, fax broadcast, and fax-on-demand. All of these tools, and many more to come, are part of the digital marketing environment. That's why it's important for you to look at *all* of the digital marketing tools—not just the Internet—and choose the ones most appropriate for your business, customers, and prospects.

- **Requires an integrated approach**: To succeed in the age of high-speed computers, databases, Internet telephony, ATMs, smart cards, and Web-browsing cellular telephones, you must approach marketing in an integrated fashion. All of the digital and online tools you use must fit together strategically. If required, your customer database must be linked to your Web site. Your voice mail must be linked to your fax-on-demand system, and e-mail must be linked to your pager network. Instead of introducing these tools incrementally, you must introduce them simultaneously, and this requires strategic planning.

- **About relationships**: Digital marketing isn't about bits and bytes, bandwidth, JAVA applets, and Web browsers—it's about people. If you only think about technology, you'll lose sight of your most valuable asset—your customers. Use digital and online technology to promote better relationships and better communication, not as a way to avoid contact with people.

These distinctions illustrate how digital marketing is different from mass marketing. But mass marketing has been with us for many decades. We all grew up under its spell. That's why many marketers apply outmoded principles to digital marketing programs—it's all they know. I developed the Strategic Digital Marketing Model to help you break away from mass-market thinking and make the leap into the digital age.

THE STRATEGIC DIGITAL MARKETING MODEL

Before you start setting up your Home Page, or start buying new computers for everyone in your office, I recommend you take the time to plan your strategy carefully. You might want to rush ahead quickly and take action, but this can be disastrous. You may end up spending a lot of time and money heading in the wrong direction. You may also adversely affect sales revenues.

This disaster actually happened to a large computer wholesale company (which, to save them embarrassment, will remain nameless). For years, the company sent us, every month by courier, a package containing dozens of catalogs featuring their computer and software products. We thought the package was extravagant, since we were not large purchasers, certainly not large enough to justify the cost of the courier. One month, however, a CD-ROM was delivered instead of the catalogs, and, at first, we thought it was a good idea. After all, it was more environmentally friendly, and a CD-ROM made sense for their target market, mostly computer stores. But we never used the CD-ROM, and neither did many of their other customers. For one reason or another, this tactic didn't work, but more ominously, the company's sales dropped by more than 40 percent within six months. They started sending out the catalogs again, but the damage was done. It took many months for their sales to return to previous levels.

The lesson to be learned, I think, is to do strategic planning and research before leaping ahead. Had the company tested the CD-ROM first, introduced it gradually, and supported it with a little bit of proactive handholding, they may have been able to make it work. But they paid the price for their lack of planning. To help you avoid a similar fate, I suggest you follow this step-by-step process.

1. **Develop a Digital Vision**: If you want to succeed, you must have a vision of your company in the digital age. This vision should look ahead at least five years into the future. I suggest you write out this vision, make it very clear in your mind, and communicate it to your partners, staff, suppliers, and, if appropriate, customers.

2 **Research Your Digital Market**: Learn the digital and online capabilities and preferences of your customers and prospects. Find out if they use the Internet before you create a Web site. Find out if they want to receive information from you by telephone, fax, e-mail, or (heaven help them) in print through the post office. Discover what kind of information they want or what value-added services they want you to provide them using digital and online technology.

3. **Use Your Database as a Collective Memory**: Databases are the single most powerful digital marketing tool. Use your customer database as the collective memory of your organization. Instead of viewing your database as simply a mailing list, use it to record all of the important information you learn about your customers and prospects. In addition, all of your other digital marketing tools, such as Web sites or voice-mail systems, should be integrated with your database.

4. **Segment Your Market**: Use your database to identify the different groups (segments) in your customer and prospect base. Determine which segments are more important than others. Target the primary segments with custom-tailored products, services, and promotions.

5. **Develop Your Creative Promotional Concept**: For each of your segments, develop a creative promotional concept that will attract the attention of your audience. Don't just put your brochure on

the Web. You need to provide something useful or valuable that will make people come to you over and over again of their own free will. In other words, your digital promotion must be something more valuable to your customer than just a commercial.

6. **Choose Your Digital Marketing Tools**: After you have completed the first five steps, assess all of the digital marketing tools available—not just the Internet and the World Wide Web. Choose the digital tools that will help you achieve your digital vision, reach your target markets, and roll out your creative promotional concepts. Although this advice seems obvious, far too many companies do not choose their digital tools wisely. They do not think strategically and usually end up very disappointed with the results.

7. **Build Your Digital Command Center**: Before you implement your digital marketing program, you need to amass the required resources, including staff, outside suppliers, hardware, and software. By planning first, you'll know exactly what resources you will need. Planning will also help you develop accurate budget forecasts.

If you wish to develop and run an effective digital marketing campaign, you must follow each of these seven steps in the order described. Unfortunately, too many people jump straight to Step 6 and choose one of the digital marketing tools without creating a long-term vision or researching their market. By failing to undertake the five key initial steps, many people fail at digital marketing. They buy the wrong computer equipment, hire the wrong consultants, and use the wrong promotional concepts. They introduce technology their customers don't want to use. They waste significant time and money by experimenting on the fly, and they possibly alienate the customers they're trying to serve. In addition, by focusing solely on technology, they run the risk of coming down with Marketing Technopia.

TECHNOPIA: AN EVER-PRESENT DANGER

Technology is everywhere in the digital age. As a consumer, you deal more and more with machines, and less and less with people. This heady march into the digital age is beneficial in many ways, but there is an underlying danger that must be addressed. Individuals or companies can become so obsessed with the wonders of technology they completely forget about their most important asset, the customer. Instead of viewing technology as a way to foster better, more meaningful relationships, they view technology as a universal panacea for their problems, or as a way to shield themselves from direct contact with customers. To illustrate this digitally induced malady, here are a few examples.

Technopia Case 1: The Database Dilettante

Recently I was invited to visit a major Internet service provider to see the benefits of their Web server technology. During the visit, the salesperson invited me to chat with the head of marketing and sales. When I entered her office, she was hunched over her computer busily working away on what appeared to be her customer database. From her demeanor, I realized right away my presence was an intrusion. Ironically, she was too busy working on her "customer" database to solicit new business. With that kind of attitude, the company didn't get my business. It was apparent they were more interested in databases than people.

Technopia Case 2: The Courage of the Early Morning Flight

Last winter, I was scheduled to fly to a speaking engagement at 6:30 in the morning. I realized I could get up later, leave at 9 a.m., and still be there in plenty of time. So I called the airline to change the reservation with the mistaken idea it would be a simple matter. After waiting on hold for 25 minutes (and listening to a recorded voice tell me over and over how important my call was), I spoke with a sales person and requested the change. They had seats available on a later flight, but they couldn't make the change on the computer. After more than an hour, and after speaking with four different people, the computer won. I had to go on the earlier flight. Naturally, I will be reluctant to use that particular airline again. I don't want a computer telling me what time to get up in the morning.

Technopia Case 3: Trapped at the Cash Register
There you are at the drug store checkout, a long line of anxious and weary shoppers behind you. You bought a dozen items to mask that you are really there to buy a medication for hemorrhoids. As the checkout person scans your merchandise, the worst thing possible happens: the product doesn't go through. She keeps trying and trying and then picks up the telephone to call the manager. Immediately, an audible moan begins to build as the people behind you start to fidget. Many minutes later the manager arrives to inspect the box of medication. She tries to scan it through and fails. Then she lifts the package into the air, for everyone to see, and says to another clerk, "Joe, how much is this jumbo box of hemorrhoid cream?" Now everyone in line is looking at you, wondering about your personal physical problems. For the next five minutes (the longest five minutes of your life) the store staff crowd around the register terminal, trying to ascertain the price of the product. Not willing to wait any longer, and not willing to suffer the smug stares of strangers, you flee the store empty-handed.

All of us have suffered through these types of situations, and they're bound to occur more often as more digital and online technology is introduced into the marketplace. Recently, I got stuck in a digital parking lot because my credit card didn't work at the exit. I was trapped and thoroughly annoyed—another victim of Technopia. So don't make the same mistake with your digital marketing program. Put people and relationships first. Use digital and online technology to foster better relationships. Keep this advice in mind as you plan and run your global digital marketing program.

CHAPTER 3

THE EIGHT GLOBAL MARKETING IMPERATIVES

Perceiving that the Great Khan took a pleasure in hearing accounts of whatever was new to him respecting the customs and manners of people, and the peculiar circumstances of distant countries, Marco Polo endeavored, wherever he went, to obtain correct information on these subjects in order to gratify the curiosity of his master.

Marco Polo's Travels
Author Unknown

In grade five social studies, I was fascinated with the exploits of Marco Polo. I was spellbound by his adventures, his long journey, and what he learned from the Chinese. I admired his ability to trade with the Chinese by learning their language and adapting to their culture. Like Marco Polo, you must also adapt. In fact, you may need to completely transform your business and how you run it. Global digital marketing is much more than simply offering your existing products and services to a larger, worldwide audience. You may need to create new products and services, and target totally new markets in different countries. So before I present the Global Digital Marketing Model, I offer you the Eight Global Marketing Imperatives.

#1: OVERCOME PERSONAL BOUNDARIES

If you want to conquer the world, you first have to conquer yourself. Be honest. In your mind, what artificial boundaries have you created? Do you think of your business as a small local operation or as a national or international venture? Do you see the boundaries of your country as a wall beyond which you can never venture? Or do you see the whole world as your marketplace? If you're honest with yourself, you'll probably discover that out of fear or habit, you've imposed an artificial boundary around your business affairs. To succeed at global marketing, you have to acknowledge these personal barriers to growth and make a commitment to expand your horizons into a larger market.

To help you develop a more global perspective, here are a few ideas that have worked for me and my company. Put a world map on the wall in your office, and choose four or five countries of interest to you. Read newspapers from these places. Look for information about them on the World Wide Web. Visit them in person or speak with people who have been there. By discovering more about other countries, cultures, and customs, you'll become more cosmopolitan in your outlook. This new knowledge will change your perspective and will gradually break down any personal boundaries you may be imposing on yourself.

#2: CONVERT ATOMS INTO BYTES

To operate effectively on a global scale, you need to change your traditional business—which may involve the processing and delivery of tangible goods and services—into a digital-age organization delivering information-based products and services. The greater amount of information you handle, and the fewer tangible items you deal with, the easier it will be to operate globally. Obviously, it's much easier and cheaper to move digital information around the globe than it is to ship products and people. For this reason, you need to "informationalize" or "digitize" your business.

To illustrate, let's say you run a transportation company that ships hazardous materials across North America. After many years, your company has amassed an invaluable knowledge base about what materials can, and cannot, be imported and exported, and about what regulatory issues are involved.

To expand globally, you have two choices. You can try to grow your business in other countries by investing in more trucks, more personnel, and other physical assets, or you can package your expertise in a digital form. For example, you can create CD-ROMs and online networks to help trucking companies around the world ship hazardous products across international borders. In other words, instead of going global with your traditional products and services, exploit the knowledge in your company and offer it to the world. The investment and risk will be much less, and the potential upside will be significantly greater as well.

So if you want to globalize your business, think about how to package your knowledge in a digital form. You can still succeed at selling tangible, nondigital goods to a global market, but the higher the information content, the greater chance your global marketing program will work. Decide for yourself the right mix between atoms and bytes for your business.

#3: DON'T COMPETE, BE UNIQUE

In the digital age, ideas make the world go round. If you want to globalize your company, ideas will make the difference. Instead of competing head-to-head with your competition, bring to market totally unique products and services. Competing directly is risky, expensive, and extremely difficult, especially in foreign countries where local business has a greater understanding of the local market. It's much better to market something unique than to compete on price, service, or perceived higher quality.

As an example, suppose you breed emus for a living (emus are large birds that look like ostriches and have become a popular farm animal).

With more than 10,000 emu livestock, you have the largest emu farms in Iowa and Alberta, and rank as one of the most successful emu breeders in North America. Now you have set your sights on a global market. You want to set up emu farms on every continent in the world, but you realize the competition is stiff out there, especially in Europe where emu breeding has also become big business. So instead of trying to compete head-to-head (or emu-to-emu), you develop the McEmu Sandwich, made from Grade A emu meat and a secret, patented recipe. McDonald's loves the idea and, within a year, it's selling the tasty burgers in more than 20,000 outlets in 50 countries. In addition, you create "The Invincible Taoist Emus," a cartoon television show starring five no-nonsense emus who battle evil. The global popularity of the show sets off an emu merchandise bonanza of coloring books, plush toys, perfumes, action figures, and everything else you can think of. Emu World, the theme park, opens to capacity crowds. A full-length, animated feature film, *Emus at Large*, sets worldwide box-office records. All of this success happens because you decided to be unique rather than going up directly against your competition.

#4: BE A SPECIALIST, NOT A GENERALIST

As a global marketer, you must present yourself as a specialist. In the past, in a small local market, you had to be a generalist. To survive, you had to offer a wide number of products or services. If you sold milk, for example, you had to also sell bread, eggs, and meat. Being a generalist made good business sense because you had a limited number of customers and needed to make as much money as possible from each one. In today's global economy, the market is almost infinite. There's no scarcity of customers. In a market of billions (and growing by millions a day), there are enough customers for almost any product or service, no matter how specialized.

From a promotional perspective, specializing also makes sense in a global market. As a specialist, you'll more easily gain the attention of your prospective customers. They'll recognize you as an expert and understand your value much more readily. It will be easier for you to communicate your unique specialty. You will, in fact, become the expert because you'll focus your attention on a particular area. Your specific knowledge will grow exponentially.

As a hypothetical scenario, let's assume you run a corporate software company. You sell a wide range of software products to major companies in Europe. You have good relationships with more than 100 of these companies and provide them with a host of different products and services. Until now, you have taken the generalist approach, and it has worked. But now you want to expand into North America and Asia. To succeed globally, you need to develop a specialty product.

Using the World Wide Web and online databases, you research the global corporate software market. You send out an e-mail questionnaire to more than 5,000 information technology (IT) officers around the world. From this inexpensive online research, you discover a gap in the market. A software program is needed that links human resources software to multimedia training software. Around the world, thousands of companies are looking for a way to integrate these two components. After a few months of development, you launch your new specialty product, the HR Training Link, and send off e-mail messages to every company in need of this specialty product. The response exceeds your wildest expectations. Within a week, more than 750 companies download the trial software module from your Web site. Around the world, you quickly become known as the expert in linking HR software with multimedia training modules. In fact, you're the only company in the world with such a product.

As you can see, specialists stand out in the chaotic and complex worldwide economy. But this doesn't mean you're destined to sell one type of product or service. You can still have a number of different business interests, but you need to specialize for each market in which you operate. In other words, you can promote yourself or your company as a specialist in a number of different market segments.

#5: SERVE A SPECIALIZED MARKET

In addition to specialized products or services, global marketing also dictates that you focus on specific, specialized markets. By this I mean specialized market segments such as emu farmers, or school teachers, or new homeowners. Once again, by specializing in a particular market, you'll become an expert in the needs of that kind of customer, and most likely, you'll be able to provide them with a higher level of value. In fact, the more specialized the market (let's say emu farmers who also raise ostriches), the more success you'll have as a global marketer.

For instance, suppose you publish sales training manuals for professionals in the financial services industry. In your national market, you serve a fairly wide market: people who sell life insurance or mutual funds or stocks, or act as financial planners. Because your local market is limited, you've been forced to serve this relatively unfocused market. To make your business global, you must narrow your sights and aim at one particular segment of the global financial services market. After researching the market, and analyzing your company's strengths, you choose a specialized global market: independent financial planners who also sell life insurance to family business owners. You develop a complete series of educational products for this worldwide audience including CD-ROMs, multimedia presentations, video and audio tapes, books, conferences, and online services. By focusing on this particular group of people, and quickly growing your knowledge of their needs, your value to them skyrockets.

#6: OPERATE IN ADVANCED DIGITAL MARKETS

As a digital marketer, you need to choose your trading partners based on their ability to operate in the digital arena. If a country has an advanced digital economy, it's a much better prospect for global marketing. If the country's digital capabilities are limited or nonexistent, so are the prospects for electronic trade. The state of a country's digital economy will determine its economic health during the next 10 to 20 years. Obviously, you want to invest in countries with a bright future. Those nations that embrace digital and online technology have the best chance of prosperity in the next century.

In Chapter 11, I present the Global Digital Marketing Index, a rating of the world's most advanced digital trading nations. This index evaluates each country's economic environment, political environment, and digital/online capabilities. Each country is given a score out of 100. The higher the number, the better the prospect for your global marketing program. Norway, for example, with a score of 88, is an excellent global marketing prospect, while China, with a rating of 21, is not, at present, a viable digital economy, and therefore is not a good global digital marketing prospect.

#7: DEVELOP INDIGENOUS DIGITAL PARTNERSHIPS

In each country where you operate, you must develop relationships with agents, distributors, importers, exporters, and other business people who will act as your local representatives. I call these Indigenous Digital Partnerships. They help you understand local customs, language, government regulations, and business practices. In effect, they are a conduit to a distinct culture. Although it may be tempting to bypass these intermediaries and go directly to the consumer, this is not the best strategy. Digital marketing is a realm where third parties such as wholesalers, brokers, and agents can easily be eliminated. However, these Indigenous Digital Partners will be key to success.

For this reason, one of your first steps in global marketing is to find and initiate relationships with these partners. Luckily, these are the kind of business people who thrive on the World Wide Web. You also need to find partners who meet your standards for professionalism, integrity, and honesty. And they must demonstrate their ability to work online in a digital environment. I will discuss this subject further in Chapter 6: Your Global Digital Market.

#8: USE TECHNOLOGY TO FOSTER GLOBAL RELATIONSHIPS

In our technology-crazed society, we're in danger of becoming slaves to the very machines that are supposed to do our bidding. In many ways, we've lost sight of the fact that technology should be a means to an end, not an end in itself. That's why I don't, for instance, answer every clarion call to install the latest version of a software program. I've spent days trying to upgrade my software only to find I need to add more RAM or more hard-drive space. Or I encounter some other problem. By the time I get it working, I've forgotten why I wanted to upgrade the software in the first place— if I actually had any reason at all.

That's why I recommend you focus on relationships, instead of technology, when you're developing digital and global marketing programs. By thinking first about people instead of machines, you'll be able to make much better decisions about what type of computer you need, what software you require, and whether you actually need any of this fancy digital equipment in the first place. It's quite simple. If you think a new technology will foster better relationships with your customers, you should probably adopt it. If you think a new technology will inhibit better relationships, or have no impact at all, you should probably reject it as unnecessary.

To be successful at global marketing, you need to use digital and online technology to bridge the distance between you and your customers, prospects, suppliers, employees, and strategic partners. The better you are at using the technology effectively, the better your relationships. And the better the relationships, the more profitable your business.

INTEGRATION OF IMPERATIVES

One important objective of your global marketing program should be to bring together all of these concepts into a complete system.

The more you integrate them, the easier it will be to operate globally. For example, if you informationalize your business, it will be easier to develop specialized products for specialized markets. If you strive to be unique, instead of striving to compete, it will be easier to be a specialist rather than merely a generalist. If you operate in advanced digital markets, it will be easier to develop profitable relationships using digital and online technology. So try to adopt all of the imperatives to some degree, rather than adopting some and ignoring the rest. How completely you adopt them depends, of course, on your situation, the culture of your company, and how quickly change can be made. As such, it is important to look at global marketing as a process, rather than as an end in itself.

CHAPTER 4

THE GLOBAL DIGITAL MARKETING MODEL

This da Gama, whose fortune it was to initiate direct European contact with the East, was a man of iron physique and surly disposition. Unlettered, brutal, and violent, he was nonetheless loyal and fearless. For some assignments, he would have been useless, but for this one he was made to order.

The Great Discoveries
Charles E. Nowell

Vasco da Gama was the first modern-era European explorer to sail around the Horn of Africa en route to India. His accomplishment opened up a nautical passage to the East for European traders and forever changed their world of business.

In the digital age, you also have the opportunity to transform the world. You have the chance to greatly expand your existing business or to create a completely new digital-age company. But you need to have a plan, and you need to develop a global digital marketing program. To assist you in this task, I've developed the Global Digital Marketing Model, a framework for planning a worldwide marketing program using digital and online technology.

The model is a step-by-step process for strategic planning and action. It's a universal structure you can apply to any kind of business, whether you have a one-person company or operate the marketing department of a major, international corporation. The model is crafted to help you think creatively and rationally, but it's not a substitute for your own common sense and experience. I encourage you to look at each concept objectively and decide for yourself how to apply it to your unique situation. It's my job to offer up the ideal global digital marketing program, but it's your job to make it work in the real world.

The Case for Strategic Planning. When I'm eager to get started on a project, it's tempting to plunge ahead and leave out important steps. This approach is usually disastrous. It's always better in the long run to take each step patiently in turn. For example, let's suppose the outside of my house needs painting. As an amateur painter, my impulse is to start painting right away. I get the job done quickly, but within a few months the new paint peels off and the house looks horrible. A professional painter, on the other hand, follows a prescribed method. He or she scrapes off the old paint, sands down the rough edges, fills the holes and blemishes, and applies a primer followed by one or two coats of paint. The professional process takes longer, but the results are significantly better. The house looks great, and the job lasts four or five years. In the end, the step-by-step approach lasts longer and is less expensive. So resist the temptation to plunge willy-nilly into global digital marketing, and follow the step-by-step model instead. Like the professional paint job, the results will be better and the planning will pay off for many years to come.

CREATE A GLOBAL DIGITAL VISION

Your first step is to develop a global vision for the digital age. What type of company do you want to build? Do you want to be an exporter or an importer? Do you want to run your company from a single office using distributors in other countries, or do you want to open offices in different locations around the world? Do you want to move away from tangible products to information-rich digital products and services? Ask yourself: What specialized products will I develop and what specialized markets will I serve? How big a company do I want to run? Do I want to increase my revenues by selling more valuable products or services, or by selling more of the same product to a greater number of customers? Do I want to bring together a team of people from around the world to create a virtual global organization? Do I want to link buyers and sellers around the world in a particular industry?

Before you move forward, you need to answer these questions and many more. This thinking requires strategic planning. You must clearly define your business objectives and your overall vision. Without a vision, you won't have a way to measure your progress. Your efforts will be aimless. With a vision, you'll know where you're headed and which actions you must take on a daily basis.

Develop Global Digital Products. To prosper in the digital age, you may need to make significant changes in the way you do business. You may need to completely change your products and services. For example, if you sell tangible goods such as toasters or emu riding apparel, consider informationalizing your product line. Develop a digital product that is related to your current business. For instance, a manufacturer of auto parts could develop an online registry for hard-to-find antique car parts. Or a briefcase retailer could develop a software program that would enable customers to customize their own briefcase and send in the order online. In other words, instead of using the World Wide Web and e-mail to hawk your existing products, think about developing new digital-age products that can be easily produced, promoted, distributed, and whose value is enhanced by using digital and online technology.

RESEARCH YOUR GLOBAL MARKET

Research is a critical but often overlooked stage in the development of a digital marketing program. Do your homework. In the long term, research will save you time and money, and help you capitalize on greater opportunities. Before you embark on a global digital marketing program, you need to:

- identify your customers and target prospects;
- divide your customer base into several distinct segments;
- create or refine your customer database;
- assess the digital and online capabilities of your customers and prospects;
- choose the countries in which you wish to operate; and
- determine the digital capabilities of your target countries.

Identify Your Customers and Prospects. You may be surprised to discover how few companies actually take time to properly identify and describe their customers in detail. Don't make the same mistake. Start by writing a definitive description of an "ideal" customer. This profile will help you assess your existing clients and prospects. Next, look at your actual clients and prospects. If they are individual consumers, describe their age, gender, income, location, lifestyle, family structure, wants, needs, likes, and dislikes. If they are businesses, describe the type of industry, company size, revenues, number of employees, type of product or service, organizational structure, and so on. In many cases, you'll discover you actually have a number of different types of customers and prospects, which leads us into the next step—segmentation.

Segment Your Market. In Chapter 6, I explain why it's important and beneficial to segment your target market into different groups. Segmentation allows you to better serve the unique needs of each group, thereby increasing the value you provide your customers on an individual basis. Segmentation also helps you identify your most profitable customer groups—the ones that most closely match your "ideal" customer profile—so you can steer your marketing efforts and money in the right direction.

Refine Your Customer Database. The database is the central tool of digital marketing. If you have an existing database, you may need to clean it up and make sure it will record the information you need, and account for your different market segments. You may also need to link your database to other digital marketing tools such as telephone IVR, e-mail, the World Wide Web, private online networks (BBS), fax broadcast, and fax-on-demand.

Target Advanced Digital Economies. The Global Digital Marketing Index (see Chapter 11) analyzes 50 major trading countries and rates their digital marketing potential. For example, the Netherlands, Luxembourg, Norway, Finland, Denmark, Canada, the United States, and Australia are excellent prospects for global digital marketing, while such countries as China, Egypt, Russia, Pakistan, and Indonesia do not yet have the conditions necessary for conducting business using digital and online technology.

Therefore, it is wise to limit your marketing efforts to countries that score high on the Index. They have vibrant and growing digital economies. They have made significant investments in computers, telecommunications, and online networks. They have a stable political climate and freedom of expression. Beyond legislating against pornography and hate propaganda, they don't try to control what their citizens can access on the Internet. They have open economies that invite foreign business and investment. They have eliminated unnecessary bureaucracy and regulation. In these digital-age countries, you'll find customers more easily and serve their needs more profitably. As well, because they have invested wisely in digital and online technology, these countries have the best prospects for future economic growth. If you make an investment in digital countries, the risks are lower and the potential for success is greater.

On the other hand, countries scoring poorly on the Index should be avoided. They have limited digital and online capabilities, so it will be difficult to do business in these countries using e-mail, the World Wide Web, CD-ROMs, fax, fax-on-demand, or even the telephone. These countries are often ruled by repressive governments that attempt to maintain control of the Internet and networked technology so as to regulate access to information. As well, these countries usually have high tariffs and other protectionist trade policies. They don't welcome foreign investors, and they put up many bureaucratic obstacles to foreign business people. Obviously, any investments made in these countries will be risky. Without a viable digital and online infrastructure, these countries have poor prospects for long-term economic growth.

CREATE GLOBAL DIGITAL PROMOTIONS

In the digital age, you must develop effective promotions to attract people to your company. Because the digital marketing environment is essentially nonintrusive, you must provide something valuable or useful that will keep your customers and prospects coming back again and again. This principle of digital marketing is even more relevant in global digital marketing. Because the distances are so vast, and the market so huge, global marketing requires promotions to draw an audience without the use of high-cost traditional mass-media promotions such as advertising, public relations, and direct mail. In Chapter 7, I offer many examples of digital promotional strategies you can use in your program.

Promotional Segmentation. To be effective, you must develop digital marketing programs for each of your target customer segments. If you have four key segments, you need to develop four distinct marketing programs. Although this sounds complicated and expensive, it does not need to be. Using digital technology, you can easily tailor your core marketing resources to suit the requirements of each group. For example, you might create a Web site for each of your segments. Each group will see a different Home Page, but the underlying information will be the same. You might have a fax newsletter going out to three different countries in three languages, or you might broadcast e-mail to eight different segments, with each segment receiving messages with similar content but with different lead paragraphs. As you can see, it is easier to create segmented marketing programs in the digital age, and they are much more effective. If you don't want to trouble yourself with added complexity, you may consider focusing solely on your most important segment. In some cases, this priority segmentation strategy is a wise move. You may profit from using your resources on one group of prospects. Either way, segmentation will help you develop a more effective global digital marketing program.

Develop Interesting Content. Now you put together the information forming the core of your digital marketing program. In most cases, marketers begin by writing the copy for their brochure or Web site. While developing company and product-specific information is important, I encourage you to go much further and gather information of specific interest to each of your customer segments. In other words, instead of writing about yourself (how great your products are, how many customers you have, how many factories you own), gather information your customers need. In our seminars and workshops, we call this exercise The Information Profiler. During the exercise, you write down 10 things your customers want to know, related to your business, but not about your business. For example, if you're a manufacturer of in-line skates, your customers will want to know:

- where to go in-line skating in their city
- where to take in-line skating lessons
- how to protect themselves from in-line skating injuries
- how to perform interesting tricks while in-line skating
- profiles of the best in-line skaters in the world
- great in-line skating tourist sites
- the history of in-line skating
- where to meet other in-line skaters
- when and where in-line skating festivals and contests are held
- worldwide in-line skating statistics

As you can see, the list does not contain any information about your company. But think about it. When was the last time you were interested in reading someone's brochure? Let's face it: brochures are boring. But truly interesting information about in-line skating, which helps budding in-line skating enthusiasts get to know the sport better—well, that's interesting. And it's this kind of information that will attract them to your digital domain. In the process, of course, they'll probably learn all about your company, which was the point of your brochure in the first place.

Develop Value-Added Digital Services. In addition to interesting information, your digital marketing promotion might include a value-added service that makes life easier or better for your customers or prospects. You might:

- set up a Web site to allow your customers to check inventory and place orders;
- provide your clients with a software program to help them make complex calculations;
- set up multimedia kiosks to help retailers present interesting presentations in their stores (perhaps an interactive DVD-powered video about in-line skating);
- establish a private online network to help industrial engineers source components for manufactured products; and
- bring together your customers and prospects as a virtual community (such as an Internet chat line about in-line skating).

In most cases, you will provide these value-added digital services free of charge to attract the attention and interest of prospective customers. However, your value-added digital service may be so useful and valuable, you could charge for it, which leads to the next concept, Revenue Digital Marketing.

Revenue Digital Marketing. Traditionally, marketing is considered an expense or an investment, but in the digital age it's possible to turn your marketing efforts into a source of revenue. For example, consider this book. It's the best marketing tool I have, and I make money selling it. I also run seminars and workshops—which are excellent marketing tools for our consulting services—and I make money giving them. While you're planning your digital marketing program, I encourage you to develop marketing tools that will also generate revenue. The trick is to invest the necessary time and money to develop marketing tools that your customers and prospects will find valuable. This means you need to develop something more substantial than a brochure. People will not pay for a simple brochure, but they might pay for a CD-ROM, a book, an online service, or a seminar.

Plot the Marketing Process. For each of your segmented promotions, you need to plan the exact process involved in the program. For example, one of your programs might consist of these steps:

Step 1: Search the World Wide Web for prospective customers and select appropriate prospects.

Step 2: Enter names, e-mail and Web site addresses into your customer database.

Step 3: Send an e-mail message to each prospect inviting them to visit your Web site. Your Web site contains a wealth of information of special interest to your prospects.

Step 4: Prospects visit your Web site and fill out a form requesting a complimentary CD-ROM. The CD-ROM contains software programs of particular use to your prospects.

Step 5: Prospects install the CD-ROM and use it to connect to your private online network.

Step 6: Prospects use the CD-ROM regularly to perform functions vital to their jobs.

Step 7: You send out regular e-mail messages to your prospects promoting additional online services available on your Web site.

Step 8: Prospects call your free worldwide 1-800 number to order your products.

Step 9: Products are shipped overnight by courier.

Step 10: Customers use your Web site to fill out warranty registration.

Step 11: Customers receive 10,000 digital credits for the order, and membership in your Loyal Membership Program.

Step 12: Customers subscribe to your PUSH channel and become ongoing, regular customers.

Working out the marketing process is vital. It helps you determine what activities are required, how many people you need, what digital and online capabilities to develop, and what results to anticipate.

SELECT YOUR GLOBAL MARKETING TOOLS

Although digital marketing can be more cost effective than mass marketing, it may often require a higher initial investment before you begin to save money. For example, sending out 5,000 e-mail messages is quite a bit cheaper than mailing out 5,000 printed newsletters. However, before you can save money on e-mail, you have to buy a computer, get an Internet connection, and set up a database and a broadcast e-mail system. You have to spend money before you can save money, and you need time and patience to develop this new capability.

Choosing the right digital tools is equally important. You don't want to invest in expensive computers, software programs, and consultants until you're convinced you really need these tools. That's why it is so important for you to look at all of the digital marketing tools available, not just the Internet and World Wide Web. Determine which ones will help you achieve your business goals, serve your customers and prospects, and fit the process you want to use to deliver your promotions. For example, you may be convinced you need to set up a Web site. But it may be more appropriate for you to set up a private online network (BBS) or develop a CD-ROM multimedia presentation for your salespeople. It might be better for you to develop a worldwide telemarketing system because most of the people in your target countries have a telephone, but they don't use the Internet. If you look at all of these options (see Chapter 8: Global Digital Technology), you will make better choices and probably save a lot of money in the long run.

Don't rely on the repair person. Most marketers don't look at all their options when it comes to digital technology. They don't know enough about the different tools available, so they rely on their computer people to tell them what to do. In this environment, the computer department reigns supreme. If the computer people think a Web site should have spinning logos, loads of JAVA applets, and all the other bells and whistles, then the site will have them, regardless of their relevance to your marketing objectives. In my opinion, relying on your computer people to direct your digital marketing program is like having your photocopier repair person design your corporate brochure. Let's be honest: most computer people don't understand marketing. They are interested in programming software, setting up hardware, and building really fast networks. They don't usually think strategically about target markets or communication goals. For this reason, marketing people should take the initiative and develop digital marketing programs, and then tell the computer people what is needed. In this way, you and your company will be the master of technology, and not its servant.

INTEGRATE YOUR GLOBAL DIGITAL MARKETING PROGRAM

A marketing program is most effective when it works like a well-oiled machine. All of the parts work in unison. All of your resources are deployed and aimed in the same direction. Little time or effort are wasted. This type of integration is only possible if you have planned every step in detail. That's why I believe strategic planning is so important, especially in the field of digital marketing. If you follow each of the steps described in the Global Digital Marketing Model, you will have:

- a global vision for your company in the digital age;
- clearly defined target customer segments in advanced digital countries;
- effective digital marketing promotions for each of your target segments; and
- a selection of the most appropriate digital and online marketing tools.

If you don't plan out your strategy carefully and you eliminate some of the steps, your digital marketing program will not be integrated. Parts will be missing. You will have a Web site, but your database will be mediocre. So take the time to work out your strategy. Don't be in such a hurry. Patience and clear thinking will be rewarded, especially in the field of digital marketing.

Now that I've made my case for strategic planning, let's get down to it. Let's move on to Section Two: Your Global Digital Marketing Program, and look at each of these steps in more detail.

YOUR GLOBAL
DIGITAL MARKETING PROGRAM

CHAPTER 5

YOUR GLOBAL
DIGITAL VISION

Columbus had covered 3,066 miles in 33 days. As far as he was concerned, the island that lay ahead of them when the sun rose was part of the Great Khan's Cathay. It was a view he held until his death. He landed that same afternoon, dressed in scarlet doublet and carrying the royal standard. Once on the beach, with inhabitants watching from the shelter of the palm, he knelt and prayed.

Ten Who Dared
Desmond Wilcox

Christopher Columbus, history's most famous global explorer, had no problem with the "vision thing." In spite of strong opposition to the contrary, he believed he could reach Cathay by sailing west across the Atlantic Ocean. He was convinced the earth was a globe and great riches lay beyond the setting sun. As we all know, Columbus had it half right. He didn't discover a new route to China, but he found something just as remarkable: the New World.

The story of Columbus illustrates the importance of having a vision. He didn't achieve his initial objective, but his vision gave him the passion and energy he needed to forge ahead, and through serendipity, his vision led him to an even greater destiny.

In the field of global digital marketing, a powerful vision serves the same purpose. If you develop clear objectives, they will give you the passion and impetus to strike out in bold new directions. Like Columbus, you may not achieve your initial goals, but by having a vision, you'll likely end up succeeding in unforeseen ways.

That's why it's vital for you to decide where you're headed in the global digital economy. Before you conceive marketing and promotional tactics, you need to articulate your long-term strategy. You need to become clear about what type of global business you want to operate. Do you want to promote your existing products and services in other countries? Do you want to transform your traditional business and develop information-age products and services? Do you want to become an importer or exporter? Do you want to bring together suppliers and customers from around the world? Do you want to serve specialized niche markets in other countries? Or do you want to give up traditional products and operate solely in the digital and online realm?

As you can imagine, answering these questions is hard work, and that's why most people never create a vision. Developing new goals requires creativity, honesty, and faith. It also requires patience. You have to stop taking care of immediate business and spend a day or two looking ahead into the future.

Sadly, many business people won't take time out for this important exercise. In our planning workshops, the participants are often reluctant at first to think about the future. The future seems too obscure, too frightening. But when the participants settle into the task, they often have an epiphany. By stepping off their day-to-day treadmill, they start to question whether they want to keep going in the same direction. Through this self-reflection, they begin to articulate a much more exciting and fulfilling future for themselves.

So, take time off from the office and think through your future path. If you work as a team, take everyone away for a one- or two-day retreat. Here are some questions for you to ponder:

- Where do we want to be in the next three to five years?
- What type of business do we want to operate?
- How will we prosper in the digital age?

AN EMBARRASSMENT OF GLOBAL RICHES

Fortunately, the emergence of a viable global economy offers almost unlimited opportunity for every kind of business, big and small. There are dozens of new national markets for you to explore, and many innovative products and services for you to develop.

Unfortunately, this abundance of possibilities presents its own problems. Such an embarrassment of global riches makes deciding which direction to pursue difficult. That's why it's important to look at many different global marketing structures and choose the right one, before you decide to move ahead. To help you in this task, here are 10 different types of companies you can operate in the global digital economy.

THE TEN GLOBAL DIGITAL MARKETING STRUCTURES

You can set up many different types of global companies, but there are 10 basic structures possible in the digital age. Within each category, there's room for a tremendous amount of latitude. For example, you can apply most of these concepts to such products as cars, toothpaste, and emu shears, or to digital-age offerings such as software, entertainment, and database information.

Study each of these approaches and determine which one is most appropriate for your business, and for your particular skills and interests. Keep in mind they are only guidelines. They may help you invent a completely new kind of global digital company.

1. The Global Digital Exporter

If you operate solely within the narrow confines of a local or national market, you have the opportunity to export existing products and services to new customers in other countries. Digital and online technologies make it much easier and less expensive for you to find and serve customers around the world using the telephone, e-mail, or the World Wide Web.

For example, if you have a company that manufactures ball bearings, you can use the Internet to find distributors and manufacturers in other countries. You don't need to conduct numerous business trips abroad. You can do most of your prospecting in cyberspace. And when you get a new customer, online technology and low-cost global telecommunications will make serving offshore clients much easier and more profitable.

In the digital age, it's also possible to set yourself up as a virtual exporter. Instead of exporting your own products, you can help other companies in your own country export their products and services using digital and online technology. For example, suppose you have experience in the medical equipment business. You can use online databases, search engines, and e-mail to source overseas customers for medical equipment suppliers in your country. In other words, instead of selling your own wares, you can make a commission exporting other people's products. This virtual exporting structure is an archetype of the digital age: an organization with little overhead, no inventory, and total flexibility.

2. The Global Digital Importer

Conversely, digital technology makes it much easier to import products into your own country. You can use the Internet and online databases to find manufacturers and exporters from other countries. For example, if you have experience in the gift-store industry, you can use global digital marketing to find exotic gift items from other countries and import them for gift stores in your country. You can act as the digital intermediary between offshore suppliers and customers in your local market. Once again, you have limited overhead, nonexistent inventory, and total flexibility.

3. The Global Digital Cross-Trader

As you become more adept at using digital technology to conduct global business, you may decide to remove yourself entirely from the constraints of your country. You may still live and work in your hometown, but you will act as an importer-exporter among countries other than your own. For example, if you live in Luxembourg, you could bring together a manufacturer in Mexico and a buyer in New Zealand. Or, you might find customers in the United States for exporters in South Africa. Your job is simply to bring people together. Remember, in the digital age, you don't have to limit yourself to your own country. You might want to live there, but you don't have to do business there.

4. The Global Digital Integrator

In this scenario, you act as a kind of international conductor. You bring together teams of specialists from different countries to develop unique products and services. Using digital and online technology, you coordinate the production process by moving digital information from one member of the team to another. Once the product is assembled, you assemble your international marketing team. And throughout the process, you never have to leave your office.

As an example, let's imagine you're the publisher of educational textbooks. Using e-mail and the World Wide Web, you find that agricultural colleges in North America are looking for a textbook on emu farming. You use the Web to find and hire writers from Spain, Ireland, and Argentina who specialize in emu-related subjects. When the writers have completed the text, you forward it over your bulletin board service (BBS) to a graphic designer in Denmark and an illustrator in California. You then send the layout by e-mail to a printer in Taiwan. When completed, the textbook, titled *How to Run a Profitable Emu Ranch,* is shipped directly to the colleges.

As you can see, this type of operation takes advantage of suppliers from all over the world and is made possible by global digital technology. Its structure allows you to use the most talented people or to find the most inexpensive suppliers. In either case, global integration gives you phenomenal flexibility and control. It also opens up numerous opportunities because you don't have to limit yourself to the talent pool within your local or regional economy.

5. The Global Community Patron

In the digital age, there are millions of different communities. However, I'm not talking about local communities defined by geography. I'm talking about communities of people who share common values, lifestyles, intellectual interests, consumer tastes, and a host of other commonalities that transcend geographical, ethnic, or other demographic boundaries. As a marketer, your customers may belong to one of these communities, and it might be a wise approach to become a sponsor or patron of this group.

For example, let's pretend you're a manufacturer of parachutes and other skydiving equipment. To increase your company's exposure, you decide to become a patron of this group. Using Web sites, chatlines, newsgroups, electronic newsletters, and online events, you bring together a community of skydivers from around the world. They share tips and stories, trade digital videos of their exploits, and participate in online discussions with skydiving celebrities.

As the sponsor of this digital community center, your company gains an outstanding reputation within the skydiving community, and sales of your products soar. Using the community patron structure to promote your existing products is only the first generation of this approach. You can also use this structure to create an entirely new global business.

For example, you can charge a fee for membership in a global association, a user's group, a fan club, a cultural appreciation center, or an international political-interest group. Once you begin attracting a lot of members, you can start selling valuable information, access to databases, travel services, events, and other things of interest to them. As long as the members of your community have a common bond and access to digital communications technology, almost anything is possible. Note: A global digital community can be developed using Web sites, private online networks, and PUSH technology, and through the telephone using 1-800 and 1-900 services. (See Chapter 8: Global Digital Technology.)

6. The Value-Added Processor

The ultimate *raison d'être* of every business is to provide value to its customers. However, being a value-added processor is something different. Within this context, you operate a company that adds value to a product or service somewhere within the production process.

For example, you may take unfinished highchairs, add finishing touches, and ship them to other countries. Or you might source a hundred different databases, analyze the data, and pass on a synthesized version of the information to a company that adds multimedia content to it. In both cases, you take raw or low-value commodities and add value to them. Although this approach sounds obvious and simplistic, it's important for you to consider this type of operation. You may be able to fulfill a specialized need within an obscure but highly lucrative global production process, either in the manufacturing or digital realm.

In my business, I've discovered hundreds of unknown, nondescript companies that make a fortune as value-added processors. For historical and economic reasons, most of them are relatively local in nature, but now, with the blossoming of a global economy, and based on the exchange of information, this type of company becomes even more viable.

7. The Niche-to-Niche Marketer

As I explained in Chapter 3, you must become a specialist to prosper in the digital age. To position yourself effectively in the vast global market, you need to offer specialized products and services to specialized market segments. Within these parameters, one approach is to sell a single product to a particular type of customer in many different countries around the world.

For example, you might export playing card sets specially designed for contract bridge players. Or you might sell a specialized electronic component used by toy manufacturers around the world.

In other words, you have a specialized product and a specialized type of customer, and you operate in many different countries.

A second related approach is to serve the needs of a very specialized niche market within a single regional economy. For example, you might operate a chemical company in California and sell a specialized type of fertilizer that only works in the unique climate of Indonesia. Or you might sell a particular brand of coffee coveted by people in Romania. These are specialized niche markets.

Once again, global digital marketing makes this type of niche-to-niche marketing possible. You can use online technology to discover and research these markets, and to promote yourself in them. In addition, bear in mind you do not need to be the actual manufacturer of products and services to operate this type of business. You can act as the digital intermediary between the manufacturers and niche markets you have unearthed.

8. The Global Digital Retailer

Using this approach, you have the goal of selling products and services online through the Internet, a private bulletin board service (BBS), or a commercial network such as America Online. Your product can be either tangible merchandise, such as books, wine, bicycles, or engine parts, or such digital offerings as software, information, databases, or online consulting services. Within this structure, many different directions are possible.

Global Online Cataloging. The first level of digital retail is establishing an online catalog of your products and services and place it on the World Wide Web. For example, if you sell quilting designs, you can create a Web site that allows customers to search for patterns they like and order them electronically.

The efficacy of this approach, now being attempted by companies in almost every consumer-product sector, is yet to be proven in the digital marketplace. At this early stage, it's still uncertain if consumers will use the Internet (or other online services) to purchase products which are readily available at local shopping outlets. In my opinion, most consumers won't use the Internet to order traditional retail store merchandise, such as mattresses, sporting goods, or clothes. They may, however, use the Internet to buy items not readily available in retail stores such as rare books, vintage wine, or antiques. It all depends on the type of products being sold.

Global Mall Manager. In this scenario, you host an online shopping center for a group of different retailers. As the mall manager, you make money by charging for "space" in the mall, or from commissions on the sale of products. It's your job to attract online shoppers for your retailers.

The success of this approach depends on how you position your mall and how well you promote it in the digital marketplace. In my opinion, an online mall must offer a specialized group of products to a specialized market.

For example, an online mall for tennis players might work. As the mall manager, you sell online space to tennis racquet manufacturers, tennis resorts, tournament promoters, and instructional video producers. To generate "traffic" you promote your site to tennis players on the Internet. They come to your Tennis Lovers Mall because they know they'll find scores of different tennis-related products and services. By putting everything together in one place, your site helps them find tennis stuff among the millions of Web sites on the Internet.

Consider the folly of a general-interest online shopping mall. In my neighborhood, for example, we have a wonderful variety of retail stores. Now someone has come up with the idea to create an online shopping center featuring the stores in the neighborhood. It's a nice idea, but it isn't going to work. Why? Because traditional retailing has nothing whatsoever to do with digital retailing. People like to shop in my local neighborhood because there are lots of different and unusual stores. Shoppers come from all over the city to wander from store to store. The atmosphere is bustling and friendly.

But on the Internet, the environment is completely different. For the most part, the goal is to find what you're looking for—quickly. There is little loyalty for a local retailer. You're not going to go to a local online mall. You're going to zoom in on a specialized one. So bear this distinction in mind if you want to set up an online shopping nexus. Pick a specialized subject area that appeals to a specific niche in the global marketplace. Don't be misled by the popular notion that what works in traditional retailing can be transferred into the digital realm.

Global Market Maker. Entrepreneurs who seize on this concept of online retailing are the most likely to succeed. In my previous book I explained how instant online access to competitive pricing information will eventually eliminate any difference in prices for a particular product on a particular day. Like the global money markets, all products and goods will be traded in a market where the customer has complete knowledge of prices. That's why I believe bargain retailing probably won't work in the digital marketing environment. If the consumer can search quickly among retailers, looking for the best price, and the retailers can easily check out the competition, prices will fall to almost the same level across the board.

Manufacturers and retailers will only be able to improve their margins by lowering their costs of production and distribution, not by charging more than the market average. Within this context, one approach is to act as a Global Market Maker. In effect, you will run a trading exchange for a particular type of product or a particular group of products. By bringing the buyers and sellers together into an open online marketplace, you will earn a commission on every transaction.

For example, you could set up an online trading post for the buying and selling of recycled waste, called The Waste Exchange. Recycling companies, which collect and sort waste into reusable raw material, will post their available stock on your site. Companies that buy recycled waste to make bottles, park benches, or industrial pallets come to the site to bid on the waste and to make deals. As the digital intermediary, you have the job of keeping the site active and facilitating the transactions. The more trading, the more commissions you make. Once again, this type of structure is ideal for the digital age. You have little overhead, no inventory, and total flexibility. In essence, your job is to combine digital technology with effective marketing techniques.

The Global Digital Auctioneer. This structure takes the Global Market Maker one step further. Instead of being the intermediary who manages transactions among buyers and sellers, you actually handle the sale of other people's products and services through an online auction format. Once again, you don't need to actually acquire these products; you simply facilitate the sales process.

Within this structure, there are two types of online auctions: the traditional version and the reverse version. In a traditional auction, buyers place bids higher and higher until only the highest bidder is left. In a reverse auction, the opening price starts high and drops steadily until someone steps in to accept the price. Both methods work extremely well in the digital marketing environment. Bidders can come from anywhere in the world, and auctions can take place 24 hours a day, 365 days a year.

As you can see, digital retailing is significantly different from its traditional antecedent. Trying to apply nondigital retailing concepts in the digital marketplace is foolhardy. If you are a retailer now, and want to build an online retailing business, you must become much more specialized in your products/services and in the market you serve. And you must take a global perspective.

9. The Global Capabilities Provider

In this scenario, you provide companies with the digital tools they need to run a global operation. You host virtual servers for voice mail, Web sites, private online bulletin boards, prepaid calling cards, Internet telephony, 1-900 services, telemarketing centers, databases, fax systems, and e-mail boxes. Instead of setting up their own costly infostructure, companies hire you to operate their network while they concentrate on making and marketing quality products and services.

For example, suppose you run a company called The Virtual Network. Your company has a client with offices in 10 different countries around the world. You provide the capabilities they need to run their global operation. In your facility, you maintain servers that host their private e-mail network, their voice mail, their corporate databases, their cross-office telecommunications, and their fax broadcast system. You own all of the equipment and software. They simply pay you a fee for maintaining the system for them. Hosting virtual global networks is a prime opportunity for digital-age entrepreneurs.

Of course, you can also become a virtual host of virtual networks. For example, you can help companies set up global networks without owning any servers of your own. You simply bring together the companies with the services bureaus and take your commission. Once again, this is a perfect digital-age company: low overhead, no inventory, and complete flexibility.

10. The Global Digital Entrepreneur

If you adopt this approach, you operate completely within the digital realm. Your products and services are totally digital in nature. You deal with information, databases, software, and multimedia content. You do not handle tangible products at all.

For example, let's say you are the owner of The Medical Knowledge Company. Your customers are medical research facilities around the world. You have a team of medical researchers in 28 countries. When medical schools or hospitals need information on a particular disease, they hire your company to search for the available data on the subject. Your job is to bring the researchers together with the medical community. When a request comes in from a hospital, you route the assignment to the appropriate researcher. You earn your revenue by marking up the fees charged by the researcher.

Once again, this type of operation represents the perfect kind of digital-age company. You have almost no overhead, no inventory, and total flexibility. You also deal exclusively with information in a digital form, which gives you the ability to work on a global scale without incurring significant communication and distribution costs.

When you work on developing your vision, think about how you can operate as a global digital entrepreneur. Ask yourself:

- What type of digital products and services can I offer?
- How can I deliver my knowledge and expertise in a digital format?
- How can I keep my overhead to a minimum and eliminate all inventory?
- How can I maintain total flexibility?

By answering these questions, you will have created the core of your vision for a global digital company.

YOUR JOURNEY TO THE NEW WORLD

Like Columbus, you need courage to achieve your vision in the digital age. You need to set sail into the unknown while others around you question your sanity. You need the fortitude to stay the course even when your crew threatens to mutiny. A clear vision will give you the passion to weather the storms and overcome the sceptics. That's why it's so important for you to spend time planning out your vision.

CHAPTER 6

YOUR GLOBAL
DIGITAL MARKET

Europe was able to exploit local situations as it found them. In some areas, like the Americas, Europeans had the advantage of surprise in their assault on indigenous societies. In the Indian Ocean, there was less surprise and more effective opposition, but Europeans found local rivalries to exploit.

The Age of Discovery
David Arnold

When European explorers set foot on new lands, they had a choice. They could develop amicable trading relationships with the Native people or subjugate them by force. As history sadly shows, most of the explorers and settlers chose the latter. They decimated the Native people, plundered everything of value, and saw conquest as their divine right. Fortunately, a handful of explorers took a higher road. They treated indigenous people as partners to help them understand the alien world they had entered. As we know, however, such enlightened self-interest was a rarity.

As a global digital marketer, you also have a choice. When you enter a new country, you can work in partnership with local business people or go it alone and market directly to the native population. If you choose the second option, you'll quickly discover how difficult it can be to deal with local customs, unfamiliar bureaucracies, and different consumer habits, not to mention other languages, currencies, and business practices. So choose the first option. As I recommend in Chapter 3, the best idea is to develop relationships with indigenous business partners. They will help you contend with the new market and act as your local representative. Like the foresighted explorers of the past, you will come to find the partnership approach to be much more beneficial.

The success of your global digital marketing program will depend, in many ways, on developing high-quality relationships with the right people in the right countries.

To find international partners for your business, you must first complete a series of strategic planning exercises to:

- choose and prioritize your most important market segments;
- define the ideal prospect for each market segment;
- pick the countries you want to enter;
- establish the structure of your database; and
- research your target markets using digital and online technology.

GLOBAL MARKET SEGMENTATION

If you want to conduct a global marketing program, you have to be very precise about your target market. In the mass-marketing era, most companies had one type of customer. They viewed their market as an amorphous mass of potential customers, each one indistinguishable from the other. In the digital age, you must choose and define your target market—or markets—by dividing it into several distinct groups.

The Market Segmentation Exercise. To segment your market, make a list of different groups you currently serve. For example, let's say you are in the hotel business. Your four main customer segments are:

A. Tourist Guests
B. Business Guests
C. Convention and Conference Organizers
D. Restaurant Customers

Using these main groups, divide them into 16 subgroups.

A. Tourist Guests
    1. Frequent Tourist Guests
    2. Occasional Tourist Guests
    3. First-time Tourist Guests
    4. Tour Group Operators

B. Business Guests
    5. Frequent Business Guests
    6. Occasional Business Guests
    7. First-time Business Guests
    8. Conference Group Guests

C. Convention and Conference Organizers
    9. Large Convention Organizers
    10. Small Conference Organizers
    11. Sales Meeting Event Organizers
    12. Major Corporate Event Organizers

D. Restaurant Customers
    13. Frequent Restaurant Customers
    14. Occasional Restaurant Customers
    15. One-time Restaurant Customers
    16. Special-event Group Customers

Now take all 16 subgroups and list them in order of priority. In other words, select the groups that are most likely to bring the most new business. For example, you could list your segments in this order:

#	Market Segment	Priority
9.	Large Convention Organizers	1
4.	Tour Group Operators	2
5.	Frequent Business Guests	3
11.	Sales Meeting Event Organizers	4
1.	Frequent Tourist Guests	5
16.	Special-event Group Restaurant Customers	6
12.	Major Corporate Event Organizers	7
6.	Occasional Business Guests	8
13.	Frequent Restaurant Customers	9
8.	Conference Group Guests	10
7.	First-time Business Guests	11
2.	Occasional Tourist Guests	12
10.	Small Conference Organizers	13
3.	First-time Tourist Guests	14
14.	Occasional Restaurant Customers	15
15.	One-time Restaurant Customers	16

Now, list the first four segments:

#	Market Segment	Priority
9.	Large Convention Organizers	1
4.	Tour Group Operators	2
5.	Frequent Business Guests	3
11.	Sales Meeting Event Organizers	4

These are the customers and prospects who represent the most potential for the future of your business. For this reason, they are the groups to which you should devote most of your time, money, and resources.

The Ideal Customer Exercise. To focus your attention on the right kind of prospect, develop a profile of the ideal customer for each of your segments. For example:

Large Convention Organizers: The ideal prospects from this group are convention organizers preparing to run a convention in your city. They are planning a convention for more than 20,000 people and need large conference facilities for seminars and workshops. They are also a well-established company with a good track record.

Tour Group Operators: The ideal prospects in this group are large tour operators planning to run frequent tours through your city. They serve a high-end clientele and are looking for high-quality accommodations for their customers.

Frequent Business Guests: These prospects are corporate executives who travel extensively and return frequently to your city.

Sales Meeting Event Organizers: These companies organize annual sales meetings for Fortune 500 companies. They are looking for a high-quality hotel to host their sales meetings.

When you have chosen your top-priority segments, and you have defined your ideal customer, you will create distinct promotion programs for each group. This will be discussed further in the next chapter, Your Global Digital Marketing Promotion.

PRIORITY GLOBAL MARKETS

Your next step is to choose the countries in which you want to do business. As will be discussed in Chapter 10, you should target countries high on the Global Digital Marketing Index. These are countries with highly developed digital economies, and political and economic conditions favorable to global business. To varying degrees, they offer:

- an affluent consumer market;
- a growing economy with low inflation;
- a high level of international trade (imports and exports);
- a stable democratic system of government;
- an efficient bureaucracy committed to promoting business;
- an environment that promotes freedom of expression;
- a modern telecommunications infrastructure;
- a high level of computer use in business and in the home; and
- a high level of Internet and online activity.

If you want to succeed at global digital marketing, start with the top 20 countries on the Global Digital Marketing Index:

Country	Score	Country	Score
The Netherlands	90	Belgium	82
Luxembourg	88	Sweden	81
Norway	88	Iceland	80
Canada	87	Ireland, Republic of	80
Finland	87	United Kingdom	78
United States	87	Singapore	77
Denmark	85	Austria	77
Switzerland	85	United Arab Emirates	75
Australia	84	France	73
New Zealand	83	Japan	73

The Country Qualifier. In this exercise, you choose your four primary target countries based on the following additional criteria:

1. What countries are most similar to your own?
2. What countries offer the best opportunities for immediate success?
3. What countries are the easiest to enter because they have languages, customs, and business practices similar to your own?
4. In what countries do you have previous experience or existing business relationships?
5. What countries will provide a base for further expansion into surrounding countries?
6. What countries are closest to you geographically?
7. In which countries will you find quality indigenous business partners?
8. What countries interest you most on a personal level?

Based on these criteria, choose the four countries you want to target in order of priority. Choosing four countries does not mean you will ignore the other possible countries on your list. However, it is wise to begin with the best prospective countries before branching out further.

At this stage, you have chosen your four market segments and your four top countries. You now know exactly who your ideal prospects are, and where you want to find them. This process may be straightforward, but you would be surprised to know how few companies clearly identify their target markets or countries.

Global Database Strategies. Databases are the fundamental digital marketing tool. Everything begins with the database. At this stage in the process, you need to prepare your database for your global digital marketing program. Your database should be set up in the following manner:

- Add fields to identify the segments to which each person belongs. Two fields may be required; one for their primary segment, and another for their subsegment.

- Create a field to store their e-mail address and their World Wide Web address (such as www.biginc.com).
- Establish the capability to broadcast e-mail and faxes from your database.
- Establish a related database which allows you to record personal visits, telephone calls, e-mails, and faxes.
- Add fields to record the answers to specific questions you want to ask your customers and prospects.
- Give everyone in your organization the ability to access the customer database over your network. The software should enable everyone to use the database at the same time.

If you take the time to clean up your database and to add powerful capabilities, your global digital marketing program will be much more effective. It will allow you to deal with more prospects and to keep track of more relevant information. It will also give you the ability to e-mail, fax, and mail custom-tailored promotional messages to each of your segments.

Global Prospect Research. At this stage, you are ready to begin searching for potential customers and business partners. Using the World Wide Web, access trading databases in each of your target countries. In Chapter 11, you will find the address of three Web sites for each of the 50 major digital countries. (You can also access a more extensive and updated list of global trading databases at www.biginc.com) On most of these sites, you can use database search engines to look for prospective customers and business partners. When you find a promising prospect, record their e-mail and Web site address in your database. If they have a Web site, bookmark their address on your browser. Remember to record the segment of each prospect.

The 50-Prospects Project. Looking for new customers and business partners is a colossal project, especially on a global scale. That's why I suggest you limit your initial search to 50 prospects for each of your four segments in a maximum of four countries. This will help you focus your efforts on quality rather than quantity.

Global Win-Win Relationships. Like the enlightened global traders of the 16th and 17th centuries, you will have much better success if you develop mutually beneficial relationships with business partners and customers in your target countries. Look for win-win opportunities that give everyone involved a share in the profits. It's not only the more ethical approach, it's also more practical. By working with indigenous business partners, you will achieve success much easier and faster in your global digital business ventures.

If you have completed all of these exercises, you are now ready to move on to the next stage of the process: Your Global Digital Marketing Promotion.

CHAPTER 7

YOUR GLOBAL DIGITAL MARKETING PROMOTION

Tradition assigns the invention of the marine compass to Amalfi, which implies it was there a magnetized needle was first attached to a circular card, with directions marked on it, and then balanced on a pin. This early compass did not bear the cardinal points of East, West, North, and South, but was divided by lines indicating the direction of eight winds.

A History of Seafaring
George F. Boss

When the explorers sailed the Seven Seas, they navigated by the stars, by watching the sun set, by reading primitive charts, and by calculating their position with quadrants, sextants, and chronometers. But their most valuable aid was the compass, first used by Mediterranean seamen in the 12th century. Fortunately, the earth has a magnetic field, a sort of built-in navigation device, because it's hard to imagine how the great explorers could have made their way around the globe were it not for the earth's magnetism.

Unfortunately, as a global digital marketer, you don't have your own built-in magnetic field. You have to generate your own magnetism to attract customers and prospects from around the world to your digital domain. The purpose of this chapter is to show you how.

Knock, Knock, Who's There? In my seminars and workshops, I always make the distinction between "sales" and "marketing." During the first few years of your business, you must spend most of your time engaged in sales. You knock on hundreds of doors, place thousands of cold calls, and give countless sales presentations. As a neophyte business owner, you must aggressively seek out prospects, and work hard to convince them to choose your products and services. These are sales techniques, and they should not be confused with marketing activities. One major objective of a strategic marketing program is to attract new customers to your business, so you don't need to make cold calls or sales presentations any more. You want people to call you or knock on your door. I call this "attractor" marketing, and it forms the fundamental basis of my promotional theories.

Getting customers to call you takes patience, investment, and strategic planning. To attract customers without sales activities, you must invest in marketing projects that may not yield immediate benefits. In fact, it might take one or two years before you start seeing a return on your investment—perhaps longer. And there's the rub. Most companies are too impatient. They want results right away, so they never invest in long-term marketing. As such, they're compelled to continue their aggressive sales programs, and they never experience the ultimate benefits of an effective marketing program.

To underline this point with a personal anecdote, consider my books. They are my best marketing tools. Since their publication, I've generated significant business from people who called me after reading them. They liked what I said in the books, and they wanted me to help them. This situation would not have occurred if I had stuck with day-to-day sales techniques. I spent more than a year researching and writing each book, and I devoted a lot of time that could have been spent making sales calls or earning money as a consultant. In other words, I had to give up immediate gratification for a much better long-term situation.

When you develop a promotional concept for your global digital marketing program, remember this distinction between sales and marketing. Keep in mind you have to be patient and invest the necessary resources, which may take several months or years to bear fruit.

But as I've stressed several times, your goal is to develop high-quality business relationships, and the process can't be rushed. If you want to graduate from knocking on doors, you have to make some sacrifices now, or you'll be caught in the sales mode indefinitely. I don't know about you, but having to make sales calls forever is one way I envision hell on earth.

ATTRACTOR GLOBAL DIGITAL MARKETING

As a nonintrusive marketplace, the digital realm requires an attractor promotional strategy. You must give people a reason to seek you out of their own free will. They have to come knocking on your door because you have something useful for them. That's why it's not sufficient to put an electronic version of your brochure on the World Wide Web. Brochure-based Web sites are boring. They don't help me in my life, either personal or business. They only act as a mouthpiece for the company that created it.

So if you want to move to a higher level of marketing, you must come up with a promotional concept to attract the right people in your target market. In general, you need to provide them with:

- information that helps them do their business better or helps them in their personal life (depending on your product/service);
- a value-added service; and
- content that entertains, educates, or informs.

For example, if you run a company that sells office furniture, you can provide your customers and prospects with:

- an online gateway to all the information on the World Wide Web about office furniture and ergonomics;
- an online database of all the office furniture suppliers on the World Wide Web;

- a software program that helps companies prepare a budget for opening a new office, including, of course, the costs for new furniture;
- a software program on CD-ROM that helps office interior designers make floor plans based on their custom specifications; and
- a CD-ROM that teaches people about the history of office furniture design.

As you can see, the information and services you provide are related to your business (office furniture supply), but they are not all about you. This is the difference. If you just talk about yourself—how great your furniture is—very few people will be interested. But if you give away something free, but valuable, you will bring your company to the attention of many more prospects. Unfortunately, most companies fail to understand this simple strategy. They only want to talk about themselves. They don't want to invest the time and money to make their marketing efforts more attractive to their target prospects.

THE FOUR LEVELS OF GLOBAL PROMOTIONS

Although marketing is usually seen as an expenditure or, at best, an investment, there is a way to make your marketing program a source of revenue. In general, marketing programs come in four levels.

Level 1: Expense Marketing. At this level, your marketing program is seen as an unwelcome expense, so you put the minimum amount of effort into it. You create low-end brochures, advertise in cheap publications, and put a few pages up on the World Wide Web. Not surprisingly, the results are poor, which reinforces your opinion that marketing is a waste of money.

Level 2: Investment Marketing. At the second level, you see marketing as an investment. You spend substantial money and time on four-color brochures and high-end advertising, and you produce a beautiful Web site with hundreds of pages, database searches, JAVA applets, and other bells and whistles. You understand marketing takes time, but you really want results now, and you spend a lot of time calculating the return on your marketing investment.

Level 3: Cost-Recovery Marketing. At this level, you produce marketing materials that you sell to your customers and prospects, such as booklets, books, videos, software, and online database services. You invest enough time and effort to raise the quality of the material so people are willing to pay for it. You don't expect to make a profit on these activities, but you recover your costs, thereby making your marketing program revenue neutral.

Level 4: Revenue Marketing. When you reach this stage, you have the best of both worlds. You are effectively promoting your existing products and services, while also making money through your marketing efforts. You offer high-quality seminars and workshops. You sell high-end books, videos, and CD-ROMs of interest to your target market. You have a Web site with a valuable database that people pay to use. In fact, your marketing program is an entirely new business. At this level, your marketing program is a natural attractor. Your customers and prospects come knocking on your door because they want what you have to offer.

Where you land on this scale from Level 1 to Level 4 depends on your attitude and your experience, and the amount of time and money you devote to it. You may need to start with Level 1, but you should plan to evolve quickly to the higher levels. To make the leap, however, you must make an initial investment to increase the quality of your promotional offerings.

TECHNOLOGY INDEPENDENCE DAY

Developing an attractor strategy also gives you independence from any particular technology. Because it's based on solving a problem or meeting a need, your strategy is not dependent on any particular digital tool such as databases, e-mail, interactive voice response (IVR), or the World Wide Web. No matter what technology comes and goes, your strategy will work. For example, let's imagine you own a company that manufactures and exports camera equipment. Professional photographers form one of your target-market groups. The objective of your global digital marketing program is to attract the attention of professional photographers in the top 20 countries in the world. Your promotional strategy is to provide these photographers with the following:

- technical information comparing all makes of professional film offered by major suppliers including Kodak, Agfa, and Fuji;
- contests and awards for professional photographers;
- a technical support group for professional photographers;
- a used photography-equipment exchange program; and
- a forum for photographers to promote their services.

To supply these services, you use a variety of marketing tools, both digital and traditional. For example, the technical information is supplied in print form, on a Web site and on a CD-ROM. The support group is run on a private online network and through an e-mail list-server. The used-equipment program is supported by classified ads in your printed newsletter and on your Web site. You also plan to create a PUSH channel for professional photographers once the technology becomes more widespread. As you can see, this promotional program is independent of digital technology. The success of the program does not depend on the popularity of the World Wide Web or CD-ROMs. You simply use the tools if they are appropriate for your target market. If a new technology comes along, such as wireless personal digital assistants (PDAs) or interactive flat-screen telephones, you will be able to use these tools to deliver your programs. Or you'll decide not to use them because they are not appropriate.

Of course, every company must develop its own promotional strategy. To help you, I've developed a series of exercises to put you in the shoes of your customers:

- The Five Question Qualifier;
- The Information Profiler;
- The Value-Added Exercise; and
- The Global Promotion Planner.

The Five Question Qualifier. This first exercise helps you identify what you need to know about your customers and prospects. For each of your target-market segments, write down five questions you want to ask every prospect you meet. For example, as a camera-equipment company, you would ask professional photographers these questions:

1. What type of photography do you do: portraits, weddings, advertising, corporate communications, journalism?
2. What photography equipment do you use?
3. Do you use any of our equipment?
4. Are you happy with the quality of your equipment?
5. Would you like more information about our programs for professional photographers, such as technical papers, peer support groups, the used-equipment exchange, and our contest/awards programs?

You ask these questions every time you encounter a new photographer and thus learn a tremendous amount about your overall customer base. You ask these questions in stores, at trade shows, over the telephone, on your Web site, or through e-mail. When you get the answers, you put the details into your customer database.

I call this exercise the Five Question Qualifier because it helps you qualify potential prospects. By asking these questions, you may be able to determine those who are not appropriate prospects, and you won't spend time or money chasing after them for business. Or you'll find those who are ideal prospects, and you'll be more confident about spending time with them. So start by developing your questions for each segment, and make sure you have a system in place to ask these questions every time you or your staff encounter a potential customer.

The Information Profiler. This exercise is very simple, but the results are very powerful. Write down 10 things your target customer wants or needs to know (related to your business), but not specifically about your business. For example, professional photographers want to know:

1. How do the different brands of professional film compare to each other?
2. How do other photographers use each type of film?
3. How do I choose between different kinds of cameras, film, lenses, and lighting equipment?
4. How do I use digital technology for professional photography?
5. What opportunities exist in other countries for professional photographers?
6. How do I light particular scenes while shooting?
7. What equipment rental companies are available in different cities around the world?
8. Where can I find photography assistants when I visit foreign cities?
9. How can I safeguard my equipment while working in extremely hot or cold climates?
10. What new technologies are being developed for professional photography?

As you can imagine, this list could go on and on. There is no end to the information needed by professional photographers. But by making this list of 10 things, your company gets a much better idea of what type of information to provide its customers and prospects. How you provide this information depends on how each individual photographer wants to receive it: in print, by fax, through a 1-900 service, on the World Wide Web, or through a CD-ROM. Regardless of the format, it's likely that photographers will be attracted to the company if you make this kind of information available. And just to underscore my point, you'll notice that none of the questions relate specifically to the company itself.

So make your own list, and do the exercise for each segment. If you have three segments, come up with 10 things for each distinct group. As you'll find, this exercise will help you develop the content for your promotional program and aid you in the selection of digital tools.

The Value-Added Exercise. In addition to useful information, you can also provide value-added services to attract the attention of your customers and prospects. These are services you give away for free, or if they are really useful, you can charge for them. For example, the photography-equipment company provides:

- a way for photographers to exchange used equipment;
- a way to exchange technical advice with other photographers;
- a database of photography assistants in foreign cities; and
- a showcase for photographers to promote their services.

All of these value-added services are provided through the company's Image Plus Program. To join, photographers complete a two-page survey (including the Five Question Qualifier). They receive software for the Image Plus Program, and a password to access the company's Web site. They also receive a printed newsletter, an annual CD-ROM directory, and a prepaid calling card giving them bonus long-distance calling time every time they rent or purchase equipment from your company.

To determine value-added services for your target markets, complete the following simple exercise. Write down 10 things (related to your business) that would be useful for your customers and prospects. For example, if you own a gourmet food company, you could provide:

- remote ordering and delivery
- a way for customers to exchange recipes with each other
- nutrition planning services
- menu planning
- food budgeting services

- cooking classes and information
- catering services
- wine-matching services
- special-needs food planning
- special-event planning

All of these value-added services, if they are provided free of charge, will attract customers and prospects to your digital domain. People who enjoy gourmet dining will come to your Web site, order your CD-ROM, call your IVR system, or access your fax-on-demand system, if you provide one or several of these valuable services.

So decide what services will help your customers and prospects. Do the exercise for each of your market segments. You'll quickly come up with dozens of ideas on how to use digital technology and traditional methods to deliver these services. It all depends, of course, upon the nature of your promotion, and the capabilities and preferences of your customers.

The Global Promotion Planner. When you have completed the three previous exercises, you are ready to put together specific promotional concepts. Write down the following and allow ample space between each heading:

> Name of Program:
> Target-Market Segment:
> The Information or Value-Added Service:
> The Tools I Will Use:
> The Process I Will Use:
> My Most Important Actions:

Looking at your two lists from the Information Profiler and the Value-Added Exercise, choose the one most likely to succeed in the marketplace. For example, the gourmet food company might complete the form in this way:

Name of Program: The Gourmet Recipe Exchange

Target-Market Segment: Cooking schools

The Information or Value-Added Service: A recipe exchange

The Tools I Will Use: Web site, e-mail, CD-ROM, fax-on-demand, print newsletter, catalog, book.

The Process I Will Use: Search the World Wide Web for cooking schools. Record e-mail and Web addresses. Enter them into database. Create Web site and recipe database. Send e-mail to cooking schools promoting the Web site. Cooking school students visit the Web site and enter the contest for best recipe. To enter, they must answer the Five Question Qualifier and post their recipe. The best recipes are added to the database for everyone to use. Visitors are also put on a list for the electronic newsletter. The newsletter is distributed once a month, listing the 10 best recipes and information about our gourmet food products. People also can access recipes using the 1-900 fax-on-demand system. Because of increased exposure through cooking schools, more people order our products through the Web site and over the telephone using our catalog. Sales increase exponentially. Earn revenue by publishing a cookbook of the best 200 recipes.

My Most Important Actions: Outline program in more detail, review available digital and online tools, determine budget.

Complete this exercise for as many different promotional concepts as you like. As I've explained, it's more effective to run a unique promotion for each of your key market segments. This may mean, for instance, you develop four different Web sites, each one catering to a different group. Or you might need to use a fax system for one group, a private network for another, and an interactive voice response system for yet another. Although this might sound more complex, custom-tailored promotions aimed at clearly defined audiences are always much more successful.

GLOBAL GREETINGS AND SALUTATIONS

All effective marketing programs follow the same basic process, and this is especially true in the global digital marketing arena. To succeed, you need the patience and skill to let your relationships evolve in the following manner.

Step 1: **Awareness.** At this stage, you make yourself known to the prospect. You do this through intrusive methods such as cold calls, advertising, direct mail, or e-mail, or you are introduced to the prospect by a third party. Your goal is to make yourself known to as many quality prospects as possible in each of your target-market segments.

Step 2: **Mutual Assessment.** You and the prospect assess each other. You try to make a good impression, and you qualify the prospect. You do this by asking five or more key questions.

Step 3: **The Bait.** If the prospect qualifies, you offer him or her useful information or a value-added service. If the prospect accepts your offer, you ask for additional information. All of this information is stored in a database. At this stage, most marketers jump immediately to the sales pitch. But it's too early in the process. The prospect is not ready to listen to your promotional song and dance. You have to be more subtle.

Step 4: **The Performance.** Now that the prospect has entered your domain, you have to demonstrate your abilities. By delivering high-quality information or a useful value-added service, the prospect gets to know you better. He or she is impressed by your abilities. A potentially long-term relationship begins.

Step 5: **Ongoing Contact.** In order to enrich the new relationship, you engage in ongoing contact. You send out e-mail, and fax and printed messages. You call them. You make appointments to see them. You maintain contact, but you do so in a relaxed and patient manner. If you are pushy, the prospect may recoil and end the relationship.

Step 6: **The First Sale.** As the prospect becomes more familiar with you and your company, he or she begins to trust you. At this point, you are most likely to make a sale. Of course, out of all your prospects, only a certain percentage of them will eventually buy. That's why you need to constantly return to Step 1: Awareness. You always need a steady stream of new, high-quality prospects.

Step 7: **Buttering Your Bread.** Some customers become important, repeat customers. They are the bread and butter of your business. To keep them happy, you provide as much service as possible to these excellent customers.

Step 8: **Helping Hands.** Referrals are your best kind of new business. You get referrals from your best customers if you provide consistent, high-quality service. Referred prospects are also more likely to buy your products and services faster because the level of trust is much higher right from the start.

Step 9: **Marketing Nirvana.** At this stage, you are extremely well known and respected in your target markets. Prospects knock on your door every day. You no longer have to make cold calls or send out unsolicited direct mail. You turn away business from nonqualified prospects. You have reached the stage of marketing nirvana.

Having the patience and skill for this process is critical to the success of any marketing program. This is especially true in global digital marketing because you will enter markets where no one has heard of you before. You will have to work harder and longer to make yourself known and to build up the needed level of trust. Luckily, digital and online technology makes initiating and nurturing relationships easier on a global scale. Because tools such as e-mail and Internet telephony are bringing down the cost of global communications, you can afford to engage in many more global relationships.

Now let's take a look at the tools of global digital marketing: global digital technology.

CHAPTER 8

GLOBAL DIGITAL TECHNOLOGY

The fifteenth century witnessed several innovations destined to have a tremendous influence—the invention of printing, the widespread introduction of gunpowder, and the advent of the three-masted ship, without which the great discoveries could never have been made.

Travel and Discovery in the Renaissance
Boise Penrose

Choosing the right technology has always played a part in the success of an exploration of discovery. During the First Age of Global Exploration, seafarers such as Columbus, Magellan, Cartier, and Balboa had to choose the right tools for each excursion. No detail was too small or inconsequential. Choosing the wrong tools could spell disaster on the open seas. Today's global explorer must be equally as diligent choosing his or her digital marketing tools. Before you set sail in cyberspace, you must understand the marketing potential of digital and online technology, and choose the right tools from a vast array of options. Choosing the wrong tools could be cataclysmic. Not only will your marketing program fail, but you may waste a lot of money on the wrong consultants, hardware, and software.

That's why I stress strategic planning. In the field of digital marketing, you may need to invest a lot of money to get your program off the ground. You can't afford to experiment with expensive equipment only to find it wasn't appropriate in the first place. That's why I also emphasize the importance of looking at all your options—not just the Internet and World Wide Web. If you look at all the tools, you'll be in the best position to make a knowledgeable decision.

In this chapter, I explain each digital tool available today for global marketing, including:

- global telecommunications;
- global online technology;
- global convergent capabilities; and
- global integration systems.

GLOBAL TELECOMMUNICATIONS

In the world today, we're witnessing a revolution in the telecommunications industry. National telecom monopolies are being dismantled. Competition is increasing and long-distance rates are falling. New services are being introduced, including global toll-free numbers, wireless personal communications services (PCS), Internet telephony, and prepaid calling cards. In addition, governments and the private sector are working together to globalize telecommunications. In February 1997, for example, the World Trade Organization hosted a summit that brought together negotiators from 70 countries. They reached an agreement that will open access to telecom markets around the world and eliminate barriers to cross-border telecom investments.

This revolution means that operating a global business will become increasingly easier and less expensive. It will lower the cost and standardize the following areas:

- long-distance calling
- inbound 1-800 and 1-900 services

- e-mail
- Internet access
- fax and fax-on-demand
- cellular and Internet access roaming
- intranet and extranet integration.

If you're going to conduct business around the world, the telecommunications revolution will have a significant impact. Of course, this revolution is not evenly distributed around the globe. Some nations are much further ahead in telecommunications, and it's important that you focus your attention on these nations. *The United Nations World Telecommunications Development Report* (1997) identified the following countries with the most telephone lines per 1,000 people:

Sweden	683	Iceland	557
United States	602	Luxembourg	553
Denmark	600	Finland	551
Switzerland	597	Norway	550
Canada	590	France	547

Interestingly, all of these countries rank high on the Global Digital Marketing Index (see Chapter 11), demonstrating once again the importance of advanced telecommunications capabilities. That's why I believe the telephone is the most important digital communications device. In every major national market, there is a much larger base of telephone users than Internet users, a significant consideration in the development of a global digital marketing program. So let's take a look at each of the digital telephone services and explore how to use them for global marketing.

Global Toll-Free Numbers. It's now possible to publish a telephone number that allows customers to call you toll-free from most major trading nations. You pay the toll and your customers are no longer reluctant to make a long-distance call. As with Internet domain names, there is a rush to secure specific, vanity-type toll-free numbers such as

1-800-Flowers or 1-800-BestEmu. If you have a particular phrase or term you want to protect and use for marketing, I recommend you register it right away, even if you don't plan to publish the number immediately. You don't want to miss out on a strategically important number. Even if you have a 1-800 or 1-888 number registered in your own country, this does not automatically give you the rights to the same number on a global scale. So register your global number today.

At press time, the following countries were offering global toll-free numbers: Canada, the United States, Australia, Belgium, Britain, Denmark, Finland, France, Germany, Ireland, the Netherlands, Norway, Sweden, Japan, Singapore, Israel, New Zealand, and Hong Kong.

International Call Centers. Think of call centers as global answering services that handle incoming calls from your customers around the world, 24 hours a day. However, international call centers do more than take messages. For example, when a customer calls a global toll-free number, inbound telemarketing representatives answer in the language of the caller. They take sales orders and field technical questions. No matter how technical your product, the representatives can be trained to deal with your customers. In most cases, call centers are a better idea than trying to set up your own facility. The large international call center firms have branch offices all over the globe and can handle most of the world's languages. Some of the more innovative firms have set up virtual call centers that route incoming calls to representatives working from their homes in countries around the globe. A person living in New Zealand who speaks German can work for a call center located in Canada. Once again, digital technology demonstrates its ability to create jobs anywhere, as long as the country has an adequate telecommunications system.

Voice Mail. If you're in business, it's likely you have voice mail. In most cases, voice mail is used solely to store messages, but it can be used for much more. You can use voice mail to:

- provide detailed information about your company and its services;
- provide late-breaking news. You can post a daily message to your voice-mail system telling callers about such things as a one-day surprise sale, a new product launch, or the opening of a new location;
- gather content for your customer database. By linking your voice-mail system directly to your customer database, you can gather additional information from existing clients and new information about prospective clients;
- provide answers to technical questions;
- provide testimonials from your most satisfied customers; and
- give people the ability to place orders using the keypad on their telephone.

Multilingual Voice Mail. Of course, all of these services and information can be provided on your voice mail in many different languages. Callers can be greeted with a message that invites them to choose the language they want to use. Which languages you use will depend, of course, on the countries you are dealing with.

1-900 Numbers. Unlike a 1-800 number, which you use to cover the long-distance calls from your customers, a 1-900 number is the opposite. The caller picks up the tab for the call and usually pays more than the long-distance fare. These services have become a popular way to peddle telephone dating services, sex chats, horoscopes, and soap opera highlights. They have also been used by telephone help-lines that charge callers for assistance with computer tech support, gardening, health care, and other services. The charges for these services appear on the caller's telephone bill.

Reverse 1-900. With a reverse 1-900 number, you pay the caller to call you. Instead of receiving a charge on his telephone bill, the caller receives a credit for calling you. Let's look at a possible scenario. You are launching a new kind of laundry detergent. You distribute a flyer in a local newspaper or through the billing envelope for the telephone company. The flyer invites people to call a reverse 1-900 number and receive a credit on their phone bill. When they make the call, they listen to an ad about the new detergent and then answer a series of questions. The more questions they answer, the more credit they receive.

Prepaid Long-Distance Calling Cards. These cards have become a booming industry around the world. You buy the cards in a store, and they entitle you to a certain amount of long-distance calling time. Once the time is used up, you throw the card away or keep it as a collector's item. In addition to their standard role as a convenience card, prepaid long-distance cards are also excellent marketing tools. For example, you can put your logo on a card that contains $50 of calling time, and distribute it to prospects. When prospects use the card to make a free long-distance call, they're greeted with a message that explains your products and services. Before they can make the free call, they have to answer a few important questions. They can also press a key to speak with a customer sales representative. You can use a calling-card promotion for almost any audience, but it's best suited for reaching well-defined markets with products and services of high value. It's also ideal for a business-to-business market in which people travel and make long-distance calls, and it's very effective when aimed at hard-to-reach prospects, such as company presidents and professionals.

Cellular and PCS Telephones. The cellular telephone industry is growing rapidly around the world. In many developing nations, wireless cellular telephones are being used instead of regular, wired telephones. In these cases, the countries are trying to leapfrog from a Third World communications system to a First World economy without laying down copper or fiber-optic cable. They are going right to wireless. The wireless telephone industry is also experiencing an explosion in options, such as personal communications services (PCS). PCS greatly expands the services offered by cellular services (including call display, call waiting, paging, Internet access, e-mail) and provides wireless communications at a price much lower than cellular. Here's a list of the countries with the most cellular telephones per thousand people:

Sweden	158
Norway	135
Finland	128
Denmark	97
United States	91
Iceland	81

Source: *The United Nations World Telecommunications Development Report* (1997).

Global Wireless Roaming. As the worldwide telecommunications industry becomes more integrated and more sophisticated, it is becoming much easier to use your cellular or PCS telephone wherever you travel. From a marketing standpoint, global roaming is important, especially if you have customers who travel frequently and you wish to keep in touch with them. For example, you might wish to give your best customers a free cellular telephone that allows you to contact them no matter where they are in the world. This proactive strategy may be well worth the expense if the client is a preferred one.

Internet Telephony. It's now possible to make long-distance calls over the Internet. Using your PC and a modem, you can call people around the world and only pay the cost of the Internet connection. At present, the technology is very crude and the quality is substandard, but it does work. It takes a little effort to set it up, and the person on the other end must have the same software and hardware. In addition, some entrepreneurs have set up services that allow you to use your regular telephone to make Internet calls. You call the service provider and your call is routed over the Internet to the destination country where it is connected again to the regular telephone system. In other words, neither you nor the person you are calling needs a computer to take advantage of low-cost Internet telephony.

Of course, the potential of this technology has the telephone companies completely spooked. They don't want people making long-distance calls for free. In some countries, such as Iceland, Internet telephony is illegal. However, this may not deter you as a global digital marketer. If you have a group of international customers you deal with regularly, or offices in different countries—and rack up astronomical telephone charges—you might consider setting them up with Internet telephony capabilities. Such a system could save you a lot of money and make your products and services more cost competitive.

Call Center/Web Integration. Some innovative companies have successfully combined the World Wide Web with their call centers. For example, let's say you sell aviation manufacturing components. Customers call up your Web site to view your online catalog of parts. They're invited to call your global toll-free number, or enter their telephone number for an immediate call-back. This gives a salesperson the opportunity to lead customers through the online catalog and immediately address any questions they may have about your products and services. In this way, you combine the personal contact of the telemarketer with the immediate visual impact of the World Wide Web. Of course, this system only works when the customer has two telephone lines, one for the Internet and one for regular calling. As such, this approach makes more sense in a business setting.

New Wine in New Wineskins. Combining a Web site with a call center is just one innovative digital marketing method that challenges current criticism that online shopping won't work. However, I think the critics have it wrong. It's true that some products will not sell well in an online setting, just as certain products don't sell well through mail order. However, techniques that combine a group of digital tools, such as the Web and call centers, may prove totally effective. It all depends on your particular business. No hard and fast rules apply. Once again, if you simply apply mass-marketing principles to the digital realm, you are bound to be disappointed. Entirely new methods will have to be found to use this technology for marketing. After all, if you put new wine in an old wineskin, it's going to taste like old wine.

Telephone Translations. As a global digital marketer, you will probably need to deal with people in languages you don't speak. Luckily, there are resources available to help you deal with translations over the telephone. AT&T has a service called Language Line. While you're speaking to your contacts, a translator comes on the line to help you. The service is offered in dozens of languages. Check out AT&T's Web site at www/att.com/languageline/.

GLOBAL ONLINE TECHNOLOGY

When I speak about global digital marketing, many people think I am talking about Internet marketing, or more specifically World Wide Web marketing. They think digital marketing is all about the Internet and all about creating a Web site. However, I stress that digital marketing is much more than just the Internet, and the Internet is much more than just the World Wide Web. This section will help to make this clear.

The World Wide Web is simply the latest manifestation of online technology, which began in the late 1970s and early 1980s when computer hobbyists hosted crude bulletin board services (BBS) in their basements. Using a PC and a couple of modems, BBS systems were usually available for free. Users shared e-mail, uploaded and downloaded digital files, and chatted with each other online. BBS systems were mostly text based and extremely slow. Then along came the big online services such as CompuServe, America Online (AOL), and Prodigy. These systems were essentially large BBS systems with thousands of subscribers. They contained hundreds of different conferences on every conceivable topic. While these services were growing in size, the Internet also began to attract many new subscribers outside its traditional base of military and academic users. Internet subscribers used different programs for e-mail, file transfers, and operating computers remotely.

However, it wasn't until the invention of the World Wide Web, in the early 1990s, that the Internet became a household name and started to attract the interest of consumers and marketers. Now we are looking at the development of other online platforms, specifically PUSH technology as demonstrated by the popular PointCast Network. In addition, the Internet is being used for making telephone calls, for accessing databases, for linking together offices and retail stores, and for running many different kinds of proprietary information systems. As such, it's important for you to realize that the online world has dozens of different platforms, including:

- e-mail
- the World Wide Web
- PUSH technology
- private online networks (BBS or groupware)
- commercial online networks such as AOL
- proprietary online networks.

Each of these online tools may have a place in your global digital marketing program. For this reason, you need to look at each tool and decide which ones are most appropriate for your business. You might discover that the World Wide Web is not the only game in town.

International E-mail Marketing. By its very nature, e-mail is a powerful online marketing tool. Unlike a Web site, which is a passive, nonintrusive medium, e-mail intrudes by being in a person's mailbox. At the very least, the receiver has to read the message's subject line before deciding to open or trash it. In fact, you can create a list with thousands of e-mail addresses, and send out a message to all of them in a matter of seconds, at virtually no cost. Imagine if all 50,000 of your customers were on an e-mail list. You wouldn't have to mail out a newsletter or a flyer. You wouldn't have to advertise in a newspaper. You could simply send out e-mail on a regular basis. Your marketing costs would shrink dramatically. So, if you haven't started adding e-mail addresses to your customer database, get started now.

The World Wide Web. From a marketing standpoint, it's vital to remember that the World Wide Web is a nonintrusive medium. To see your site, people have to seek it out. It's not like a television ad that interrupts your favorite show or a billboard that suddenly comes into view on the highway. If people don't want to see your site, you can't force it on them. For this reason, you have to make your site attractive enough so people will seek it out on their own. Your site has to be a magnet that pulls people into your digital domain. In general, if you take the advertising approach and put your brochure online, people are going to stay away. Let's face it: brochures are boring. But if you put some entertaining, interesting, and useful information on the Web, your customers and prospects will keep coming back. Here are a few hints on how to make your Web site a powerful marketing tool.

- **Provide a value-added function**: Your site will be popular if you help people perform a function faster and easier than they can with traditional methods. Instead of putting your brochure online, think of a function that could be performed electronically by your customers. If you're a retailer with a lot of repeat business, allow your customers to browse your merchandise and make purchases online. Let them perform complex calculations quickly. Help them find things or get in touch with people. Give them the ability to input data and receive a complete report. All of these services will attract customers and prospects to your site.

- **Think public relations, not advertising**: Instead of putting your brochure online, provide a valuable public service. If you're in the travel business, run a site offering tips about travel in foreign countries. If you have a waste disposal company, feature advice on how to dispose of dangerous chemicals. If you have a scuba diving company, provide a complete guide to all the scuba diving locations in the Caribbean. Before you put up your Web site, think about the subject matter in which you're an expert, and build your site around it. The result will be greater interest in your site and more repeat visitors.

- **Be entertaining**: To encourage people to return time and time again, entertain them. Publish humorous or insightful stories. Provide entertaining video or sound clips. Give them something to laugh or cry about, and update the site regularly.

- **Use nonpartisan information**: Your Web site can provide a valuable service to your customers by offering nonpartisan information about every facet of your industry. If you're in the hospitality business, offer a list of all the hotels and restaurants in your market, even those of your competitors. If you run a campground and are recruiting campers, provide a list of all the camps, and links to their sites. If you're an automotive dealer, set up a site with a search function that allows your visitors to type in their needs and get a report on all the cars that meet those requirements—not just the cars you sell. This might sound like giving the house away, but think about it; if you set up a nonpartisan site and give out valuable information, people will keep coming back.

- **Include a survey form**: Every Web site should have a place where people can leave their name and e-mail address. You want to find out as much as you can about each visitor. To encourage visitors to leave their names, give them an incentive. Hold a contest, or offer some other compensation for filling out the form. You can offer them a free mouse pad or free software to download. Ask if they want to join your e-mail list and receive regular information about your Web site's subject area.

- **Give visitors a digital present**: Give your Web visitors a digital present before they leave your site. This could be a screen saver, a software program, a computer game, or any other small promotional item.

Assume the Producer's Role. Unfortunately, most sites on the Internet are simply an electronic brochure. Either their owners don't understand the nonintrusive nature of the Web, or they are not prepared to create their own content. They are not prepared to be producers or spend the time and money needed to develop interesting and useful content. This tendency is a holdover from the mass-marketing era when someone else took care of the content. For example, when you take out an ad in a magazine, you're not expected to also write the articles. If you run a television ad, you don't have to create the sitcom or the movie-of-the-week. But in the digital age, you have to be prepared to assume the role of the producer.

Global Web Considerations. As a global digital marketer, you may need to produce e-mail and Web sites that serve a number of different countries in several languages. Although digital and online technology makes this possible, operating in multiple countries will add to the complexity of the process. You will need to consider two issues closely: access and translation.

- **Global Web access**: Although the Internet is an international and an electronic medium, access to Web sites is slowed down by distance. That's because overseas users must travel through many more routers and switches before they reach your site. If there is a slowdown at any one of the routers, your site may become painfully slow or inaccessible. To combat the distance issue, many multinational sites are "mirrored" in different countries. This means the Web site is reproduced and stored on servers closer to the end user. This speeds up access to the site in local markets.

- **Global translations**: Translating Web sites and e-mail messages can be a laborious and time-consuming endeavor, but there are software programs that can facilitate global translations. For example, there is a product called Globalink E-mail Translator for Eudora. The program translates e-mail messages made with Eudora into French, Spanish, German, and Italian. There are also translation services that combine software and human assistance. One such service is called Uni-Verse (www.uni-verse.com). For $20, plus $10 a month, you can use the service to translate messages and for chatting online in different languages. To use the service, you download the software called "Diplomat" and connect to the Uni-Verse Web site.

- **Global Web tastes and vernaculars**: In addition to translations, you must also make sure your multilingual Web site accounts for local slang and word usage. For example, the term "Home Page" is translated as "pagina inicial" or "first page" in Spanish, and "page d'accueil" or "welcome page" in French. You may also need to design your sites to appeal to the graphical tastes of local markets. For example, the McDonald's site in the United States is done in golds and reds, while the Japanese McDonald's site employs browns and pinks.

Note: The scope of this book does not allow for the detailed description of local tastes, customs, and business practices. However, you will find a number of excellent books on this subject listed in the bibliography.

Bulletin Board Service (BBS). A BBS is different from a Web site in one fundamental way: as a rule, a Web site is something you look at, while a BBS is something in which you participate. If you're interested in getting people together to interact as a group, a BBS may be more appropriate than a Web site. From a marketing perspective, a BBS has many important features that distinguish it from a Web site.

- **Access through both the Internet and regular telephone lines**: Your subscribers can dial in through their Internet account or through regular telephone lines. Either way, they have access to your BBS. This is not possible with a Web site.

- **Promotion as a unique product**: Unlike a Web site, which is just one in a few million, the packaging of a BBS gives it the quality of a distinct product and service.

- **Easy to administer**: Unlike a Web site, you do not need to constantly add content to the BBS. If you establish a core group of active users, they will generate the content and make the BBS interesting. As well, if you need to upload content, you simply send an e-mail message.

- **Your internal e-mail system:** In my company, my customer BBS also runs as our internal e-mail system. All my clients, suppliers, and associates are connected to it. When a client sends me an e-mail message, it appears instantly on my computer. It's as if we are all working in the same office, using the same network. You can see how this brings me closer to my clients.

- **A direct global connection:** A BBS system can help you integrate your business more closely with your customers and prospects. You can hook up your customers to the BBS and give them a user ID and a password. If they want to send you a file, or vice versa, the file can be transferred immediately. It's much faster and easier than sending a regular Internet e-mail message with an attachment. A file sent through the BBS is like a direct courier rather than postal delivery. The customer finds the BBS to be a much more direct connection to your company, an important consideration in a global marketplace where the sense of isolation and great distances can hinder the development of ongoing business relationships.

- **Multilingual BBS systems:** Like most software programs and Web browsers, BBS software programs are available in dozens of different languages. This means all of the interface instructions can be delivered to users in their native language. However, you are still faced with translating any content you put on the BBS.

- **Cross-border chatting:** One feature of a BBS that has also made its way onto the Web is online chatting. This gives a group of people the ability to talk to each other live online. In the past, you needed to chat with people in your own language, but now there are software programs that will automatically translate chats from one language to another instantly. One such program is called *Barcelona*. It allows Internet users to chat in six languages: English, Spanish, French, German, Italian, and Portuguese.

Commercial Online Services. There are two reasons why you might want to get involved with a commercial online service such as America Online, CompuServe, or the Microsoft Network. As a global digital marketer, you can use these services to connect to the Internet in all major trading countries. CompuServe Network Services, for example, provides almost 200 access points in 150 countries. When you are doing business in a country such as Argentina, you can connect to the Internet through a local CompuServe number and check your e-mail, surf the Web, or connect to a computer in your office. Other companies such as AT&T, IBM, and a consortium called iPass offer similar roaming access services.

In addition to roaming access, commercial online services have millions of subscribers. This audience represents a huge market. You can place banner advertising to attract them or become actively involved in one of their online conferences. With 10 million subscribers, AOL is now the undisputed leader of commercial online services. Globally, AOL runs a number of country-specific services in Canada, Germany, France, the United Kingdom, Sweden, Japan, and Australia. If you are marketing in these countries, you might consider getting involved with these services.

PUSH Technology. Just when you thought the World Wide Web was the last word in online technology, along comes PUSH technology. In essence, the technology works like this. Instead of going out on the Web and getting information, PUSH technology sends it to your computer. This is the principle behind the PointCast Network (PCN), the first viable example of a PUSH "channel." As a free subscriber, you download the PointCast software and choose the information you want to receive. On a regular basis, or on demand, the network sends you customized information about sports, weather, companies, and a host of other topics. Instead of going to look for the information, it gets sent to you. In many ways, PUSH technology is a combination of the Web and television. You choose what topics you want to see, but the content is sent to you automatically. You don't have to go looking for it. The system is also much richer visually because it overcomes the bandwidth limitations of the Web. One area of opportunity for marketers is to advertise on one of these channels (advertising supports the free subscriptions). In addition to the PointCast Network, America Online has a PUSH channel called "Driveway," Microsoft has the "Active Desktop" system, and NetScape has a channel called "InBox Direct." Each of these companies is vying to establish the PUSH standard.

- **Your own global PUSH channel:** If you have loyal customers who need to get information from you constantly, you might be wise to set up a PUSH channel. If you own an investment company, for example, you could set up a channel for your investors. Every hour, the channel broadcasts information to investors: stock quotes, graphs, company news, and investing advice. To set up a channel, you will need to purchase one of the proprietary PUSH technology platforms such as *Marimba* or *InCommon*. The software gives you the ability to create content and broadcast it over the Internet to people who have subscribed to your channel. For the most part, this strategy will work best if you are in a position to proactively set up your customers on the channel. From my experience, configuring your computer to accept a PUSH channel is difficult and fraught with bugs. However, as a global digital marketer, you need to keep an eye on PUSH technology. It has the potential to be the next fad on the Internet.

GLOBAL CONVERGENT CAPABILITIES

As a global digital marketer, you will be dealing with many different countries, with many different people, who have their own unique way of communicating, not just with respect to language, but also with respect to their digital and online capabilities and preferences.

Depending on your market, you may need to communicate with your customers using voice telephone (land line or wireless), by e-mail, by fax, or through the World Wide Web. Luckily, thanks to a convergence of all these technologies, you can conduct digital marketing with your customers and prospects, even if they don't have a telephone. In the digital age, you can:

- send an e-mail to someone's voice-mail box;
- receive a fax sent by e-mail or send an e-mail through your fax machine;
- listen to your e-mail messages over your cellular telephone;
- read e-mail messages from your voice-mail box;
- send an e-mail to a customer's pager;
- distribute letters through the post office sent by e-mail; and
- perform dozens of other operations.

From the standpoint of global digital marketing, this convergence is empowering. It means you can conduct business almost anywhere in the world, and serve almost any market, using digital and online technology. If you are in Luxembourg, you can check your e-mail messages using your PCN telephone. If you want to send direct mail to your customers in Sweden, you can send it out by e-mail through the Swedish post office. When you want to distribute faxes to companies in Singapore, you can send them out through your e-mail account. The possibilities are endless.

GLOBAL INTEGRATION SYSTEMS

If your digital vision is to create a virtual global organization, digital and online technology will make it possible. Using low-cost Internet connections in each of your host countries, you can connect your offices, your customers, and your suppliers through a global integrated network. In addition, you do not need to invest in any server hardware or software; you can hire service bureaus to host your network instead. For example, let's say you want to connect 20 international offices together over a private online network (BBS). You hire a service provider to host the BBS server and have each office connect to the system through local Internet service providers (ISP). Through this network, you can exchange files, send and receive e-mails, and do a myriad of other things.

As another example, let's say you want to connect all of your international suppliers to an ordering database system. You can set up a database server in your head office (or at the office of a service provider) and have the suppliers connect to it over the Web. In both cases, you do not need to invest in any server technology or spend a lot of money on long-distance tolls. You can run the entire operation over the Internet. (Note: Although the Internet is an ideal low-cost solution, the Net is often slow when you need it to be fast. That's why many larger organizations choose to pay for direct data lines. Retailers, for example, often need uninterrupted speed and can't tolerate the traffic jams that often build up on the Internet.)

Although the size of this book does not allow for a full, technically detailed discussion of global integration systems, it's useful for you to understand the general possibilities. As you envision your global organization, it's helpful to know you can set up a worldwide operation using the Internet and virtual hosting services. For example, if you plan to market to a group of people who use faxes, but not the Internet, it's helpful to know there are companies that can broadcast faxes for you over the Internet, thereby lowering long-distance costs. (For an example of this technology, visit FaxNet at www.faxnet.net).

WISE DIGITAL CHOICES

This chapter shows that the tools available for digital marketing are almost endless in variety and complexity, and new tools are also being introduced every day! Because of this, choosing the right tools is extremely important. You don't want to spend significant dollars on computers and software if you're not sure you're investing in the right stuff. That's why it's so important to work carefully through your strategy first. If you've developed a vision for your company, researched your global market, and created an enticing digital promotion, you will be in a much better position to make wise digital choices.

In the next chapter, Integrated Global Digital Marketing, we will look at how to put all of these concepts together.

CHAPTER 9

INTEGRATED GLOBAL
DIGITAL MARKETING

Magellan's ship Victoria *sailed 43,380 sea-miles on her voyage of circumnavigation. For the first time, a voyage had been made in all seasons and weather in search of trade. The ship had held her course despite all the hazards of navigation; she had returned safely to port, laden with a full cargo of spices brought from the other side of the world.*

Men and Ships around Cape Horn
Jean Randier

As the story goes, Magellan died on the Pacific island of Macatan, many months before his crew completed the first circumnavigation of the earth. By a circuitous route, the crew had logged almost twice the circumference of the planet and had returned home loaded with marketable cargo from distant lands. After many centuries of trial and error, human ingenuity, passion, perseverance, and courage came together to realize this historic achievement.

As a global digital marketer, it's also time for you to put it all together. If you have been following this book step-by-step, you are ready to develop and implement a global digital marketing program. To work, however, your program must be an integrated system. All of the pieces must fit together. You must:

- have a vision for the future of your company in the global marketplace;
- focus on a well-defined group of customers in digitally advanced countries;
- use a promotional concept that attracts the attention of your target prospects; and
- employ the most appropriate digital and online marketing technology.

For the most part, your global digital marketing plan must be straightforward, practical, and based on common sense. It must take into account the realities of the business world, the limited resources of your company, and the fallibility of human nature. However, linear thinking will only take you so far. Your global digital marketing program must also be a work of art. For this reason, the most important part of the planning process—the part that separates mediocre marketing programs from stellar ones—is innovation. Ideas. Bright, smart, unique, and interesting ideas. That's what's going to attract attention to your company. Not the same old thing. Not what everyone else is doing, but something so new, so unique, that people will prick up their ears and take notice. It's a big idea that will make all the difference.

When you're planning your global digital marketing program, encourage creativity and brainstorming. Come up with completely new and different ideas. To help you in this task—to get creative adrenalin coursing through your veins—here are five fantastic and hypothetical scenarios.

THE EMU MEDICINE MAN: GLOBAL EXPORTER

One morning in Alice Springs, Australia, veterinarian Peiter Ponka came up with a brilliant idea. For more than a decade, Ponka had been working with local emu farmers helping them keep their livestock healthy. He had developed special equipment for diagnosing and treating ailing emus. After reading *Global Marketing for the Digital Age*, Ponka developed a global vision to export a diagnostic system that veterinarians around the world could use to treat their local emus.

That afternoon, Ponka set to work on his global digital marketing program. Doing the Market Segmentation Exercise and the Country Qualifier Exercise, he decided to sell his equipment through veterinarian supply companies in the top 10 digital economies: The Netherlands, Luxembourg, Norway, Canada, Finland, the United States, Denmark, Switzerland, Australia, and New Zealand. Ponka realized vet supply companies in these countries would be more likely to use digital technology in their work. Using the World Wide Web, Ponka searched Web sites and databases looking for prospective business partners. In one day, he found more than 100 prospects and entered their names and e-mail addresses into his database. He became certain that a worldwide market was available to him on the Internet.

To attract the attention of his prospective customers, Ponka spent three weeks building a Web site called Emu Health Care Online. Using freely distributed data gleaned from hundreds of databases and Web sites, Ponka built an impressive collection of research articles covering almost every possible emu disease and malady. He also created a comprehensive gateway linked to more than 500 Web sites of interest to vets and veterinarian supply companies.

Ponka launched his global digital marketing program by sending out an e-mail broadcast to the prospects in his database. He invited them to browse Emu Health Care Online to:

- review the library of research articles;
- exchange information with vets and veterinarian supply companies around the world;
- use the gateway to reach related sites on the Web; and
- subscribe to a free electronic newsletter called
  The Emu Caregiver.

Of course, by visiting the site, Ponka's prospects could also learn more about The Emu Monitor, a state-of-the-art device for examining and treating emus. The handheld device is used to monitor an emu's heart rate, respiratory system, and brain-wave activity. It also comes with a blood-sampling attachment. After an examination, the vet returns from the field and places the device in a docking station attached to a computer. The monitor transmits the data over the Internet to Ponka's online server in Australia where the information is analyzed. Within minutes the diagnosis and treatment recommendation are sent back to the veterinarian by e-mail. Should vets wish to speak with The Emu Medicine Man directly, they dial through a local Internet telephone service provider to Australia, and pay for his one-to-one consultation on a per-minute basis.

Within six months, Ponka had five business partners in the top 10 digital countries. Through their sales efforts, they sold Ponka's emu monitor to more than 25 vets, and more than 500 emus were saved from premature demise. Looking ahead to the future, Ponka has a even broader global digital vision. Using his digital capabilities and global marketing network, Ponka plans to establish the Worldwide Center for Emu Disease Control. The center will track the spread of emu-related diseases around the world and, he hopes, eradicate the scourge of many unnecessary emu deaths. All thanks to global digital marketing.

THE GLOBAL DIGITAL ART DEALER

Carol Canvas, chief executive officer of Global Art Inc., looks out over Manhattan from her penthouse, thinking about her triumph as a global digital marketer.

It all started in 1998, after she reflected on some of the concepts she read about in *Global Marketing for the Digital Age*. Canvas decided to become a global digital cross-trader. She decided to specialize in leasing and selling artwork, produced by artists in many different countries, to banks and other financial institutions around the world. Using the World Wide Web, e-mail, and low-cost telecommunications systems, she established business relationships with hundreds of art gallery owners in the top 20 digital countries. She created a private online art gallery—available by invitation only—featuring more than 1,500 international artists. Interior designers, architects, and buyers for financial institutions subscribed to the site and used it to search for just the right work of art for their lobbies and boardrooms. When artwork was leased or purchased, it was shipped by courier from the country of origin to the customer. On any given day, more than 500 works of art were shipped between the 20 different countries. Carol Canvas made her money by tripling the royalty paid to the artist.

But the success of her traditional cross-trading business was not enough. Carol Canvas had an even bigger and better idea, a digital-age idea. Using her profits, she created the Global Digital Art Network. Using revolutionary display technology, she installed 300 gigantic digital murals in the lobby of banks, insurance companies, museums, and airports around the world. Regularly, new high-resolution works of digital art were transmitted over the Internet to these displays. To select a new digital mural for their lobby, clients simply visited the company's Web site to browse the online gallery. They could even choose a complete program of artwork to appear on a given schedule over upcoming days or months. And because of advances in high-definition, large-scale display technology, the viewing public could barely tell the difference between the digital art and the real thing. By using digital and online technology, and by linking artists and customers together from different countries, Carol Canvas became one of the most influential and successful art dealers in the world.

Today, gazing down Park Avenue, Carol Canvas has an even more ambitious global digital vision. In the next year, she will set up a global network of public hologram displays. Hologram producers from countries around the globe will produce three-dimensional sculptures, which will be transmitted over the Internet to 2,000 shopping malls and public squares in 50 countries. As in the case of the digital art, clients will choose holograms by ordering them from a wide selection on the Online Hologram Web site. In addition to her vision of hologram world domination, our intrepid global digital cross-trader envisions a day when everyone will put up digital art displays in their living rooms, install hologram projection units in their bedrooms, and order digital art for their homes through the Internet. And beautifully, payment for the online leasing will be automatically debited from the customer's bank account. Once again, all thanks to global digital marketing.

NAUTICAL NET: GLOBAL DIGITAL RETAILER

As one of the world's leading global digital retailers, Fredric Boomvang is also glad he read *Global Marketing for the Digital Age*. The book gave him the idea to launch Nautical Net, a digital retail outlet for the global sailing community. Since its maiden voyage in 1998, Nautical Net has lured more than 25,000 customers from more than 35 countries. They subscribe to the Nautical Net Web site, PUSH channel, and electronic newsletter in order to buy and sell boats, nautical parts, and supplies, to book boat charters, and everything else on the Seven Seas.

From his 45-foot yacht in Amsterdam, Boomvang used the World Wide Web to find business partners in the top 30 digital countries listed in the Global Digital Marketing Index. He searched online databases looking for people working in the sailing industry in each of his target countries. He set up an arrangement with them to sell advertising and editorial space to yacht builders, charter companies, and local sailors looking to sell their boats. To attract subscribers to Nautical Net, Boomvang enlisted sailing associations and yacht clubs as business partners. He provided them with rechargeable, prepaid calling cards to sell to their members. When a sailor buys the card, the association or club receives an immediate commission, and an ongoing royalty every time the user replenishes the card. In addition to low rates on long distance, the card also gives users instant membership in Nautical Net. Every time they buy merchandise on the system, or buy digital space to sell something themselves, they receive more credit on their calling card.

As the captain of Nautical Net, Boomvang is perched in an enviable position. He has a completely flexible business with low overhead and no inventory. All nautical products bought and sold over the system are shipped directly from the owner to the customer. Boomvang receives a commission on every purchase and makes a fortune from the prepaid calling cards. He has also developed a PUSH channel, which is quickly becoming *the* broadcast network for the worldwide sailing industry. The PUSH channel broadcasts a steady stream of multimedia information to personal computers, Web TV units, digital display telephones, pagers, and handheld, wireless personal digital assistants (PDAs). The PUSH channel is received by subscribers at home, at yacht clubs, in offices, and on yachts sailing across the ocean. It broadcasts worldwide sailing conditions, yacht racing results, sailing tips, and a universe of other nautical news.

Like the great sailors of yesteryear, Boomvang dreams of even greater glory on the digital seas. He is working with three major yacht manufacturers to develop the Mariner's Manufacturing System, which will enable yachtsmen to design and customize their own yachts using proprietary software and online technology. Sailors from anywhere in the world will be able to design their own yacht and watch it being built online. They will also be able to test the performance and handling of their design using test-drive simulation software.

Boomvang is excited about these future opportunities. His prospects are bright and his sails are trim because he had a global vision, aimed his business at a specialized market, and used digital and online technology in an integrated, strategic fashion.

THE VECTOR BUREAU: GLOBAL CAPABILITIES PROVIDER

To capitalize on the global digital revolution, Mohammed Ali Servo of the United Arab Emirates decided to build a company to provide the virtual hosting of Web sites, BBS systems, e-mail and fax mailboxes, database warehouses, voice mail, Internet telephony, and PUSH channels. Called The Vector Bureau, the company helps global digital entrepreneurs run worldwide companies. They hire The Vector Bureau to provide them with global capabilities so they don't have to invest in expensive fixed overhead such as computers, servers, software, and telecommunications lines, not to mention maintenance and development staff.

One of Servo's clients is TransNet Customs Brokers. TransNet hired his company to link its 28 offices in 17 countries. From his command facility in the Jebel Ali Free Zone, just outside Dubai, Servo hosts TransNet's international voice, fax, and e-mail system. In addition, The Vector Bureau hosts the company's private online network, its Web site and intranet, and most important, its long-distance telecommunications system. To save money, most of the telephone calls between TransNet employees are routed through the Internet telephone switches maintained by Servo's company.

TransNet benefits greatly from its relationship with The Vector Bureau. Its computer and telecommunications costs have dropped by 75 percent. TransNet doesn't have to worry about maintaining or upgrading the equipment; it's handled by The Vector Bureau, 24 hours a day. And TransNet can expand into other countries at a much lower cost and has the flexibility to add new services as they come on stream.

Since proving the benefits of virtual hosting, Servo's company has grown exponentially. More than 50 companies run their global digital systems through The Vector Bureau in the United Arab Emirates. By pooling their resources within one company, they benefit from the research and capital investments made by Servo's firm. They are also able to concentrate on running their business, not on maintaining complex hardware and software.

DR. MANUEL PINCE-NEZ: GLOBAL DIGITAL ENTREPRENEUR

Dr. Manuel Pince-nez is another pleased reader of *Global Marketing for the Digital Age*. Before he read the book, Dr. Pince-nez ran a one-doctor medical research center in Santiago, Chile. After completing the book, he woke up in the middle of the night with a startling global digital vision. He would create the Medical Research Network, and as we know, the rest is history.

Basing his strategic planning on the Global Digital Marketing Model, Dr. Pince-nez decided to bring together medical researchers from around the world using digital and online technology. Using the World Wide Web, he found more than 200 researchers in 28 countries who were interested in working freelance through The Medical Research Network. To attract the interest of his clients—hospitals, medical schools, and research institutes—Dr. Pince-nez compiled an extensive database of the existing medical literature on the World Wide Web. He sent out hundreds of e-mail messages inviting doctors, professors, and researchers to check out the site, and to learn about the Medical Research Network. He also enlisted the help of business partners in each target country to sell the benefits of the network to local physicians.

As a complete digital operation, the company has grown quickly. When Dr. Pince-nez receives a contract for a research project, he directs the work to the most qualified researcher on his network. It doesn't matter if the researcher lives in Taiwan, Finland, Argentina, or South Africa. Whoever is the most qualified gets the job. Dr. Pince-nez makes his money by marking up the fees charged by the researcher. Over time, The Medical Research Network has developed a reputation for excellent work, and contracts flood in from around the world. In some cases, 20 or 30 researchers, scattered across the globe, work together on a project, linked by the company's private online network.

As a global digital entrepreneur, Dr. Pince-nez has the perfect company for the digital age. He has very little overhead and no fixed staffing costs, except for a small head-office administration team. He has carved out a specialized niche in a global marketplace. He is using digital and online technology to lower costs and enhance his customer service. He is providing a high-quality service at a relatively low cost, and he has the flexibility to quickly change and transform his business. And most important, he operates strictly in the digital realm. He only handles the processing and exchange of digital information, and his high profit margin reflects the benefit of this approach. Once again, all thanks to global digital marketing.

TO INFINITY AND BEYOND

Everything and anything is possible in the global digital age. Using today's tools of global exploration and discovery, you can attempt what was once not even imagined. You can dream big dreams and take giant leaps. All it takes is imagination, a hearty dose of courage, and a strong vision backed up by a sound strategic plan. If you have been diligently following the process outlined in this book, you are probably eager to set sail on your global digital voyage. However, I invite you to keep your ship tied to the dock for just a few moments longer. Before you cast off, I suggest you read the next section, The Global Digital Marketing Environment, to get a complete perspective on the digital world out there beyond your local port of call.

THE GLOBAL DIGITAL MARKETING ENVIRONMENT

CHAPTER 10

THE NEW DIGITAL
WORLD ORDER

The nations who were to dominate modern European history organized their policies around the simple idea that confined economic thought from the beginning of history: all wealth was limited; one nation's gain was another's loss... These assumptions ruled western Europe from the fifteenth till the eighteenth centuries. With stronger armies and more potent navies, your nation could reach for an ever-larger share of the world's treasures.

The Discoverers
Daniel J. Boorstin

Mercantilism was an economic doctrine that prevailed following the discovery of the New World. Under the mercantile model, nations accumulate wealth at the expense of other countries. To prosper, a nation wields military might and expands its influence through imperialism and colonialism. Trade between nations is considered foolhardy.

Many aspects of mercantilism still dominate our economic worldview. For the most part, nations still compete against each other, even with their coziest trading partners. Countries still seek wealth by expanding their military and cultural dominance over other nations. And economists still report trade surpluses and deficits with an air of reverence.

Indeed, the mercantile world order is still with us, even in an age of free trade and globalization. But a great transformation is about to take place. With the ascendency of digital and online technology around the world, new radically different factors will determine the economic well-being of nations. I call this change the New Digital World Order. The economic fate of nations will be determined by the vibrancy of their digital economy, and the success of their digital economy will be determined by the country's commitment to democracy and freedom of expression. That's why I believe many repressive countries, which have prospered to some extent within the mercantile and industrial models, will have to change their political systems to succeed in the digital age of the 21st century.

Consider China. In China, if you want to access the World Wide Web, you go to an Internet salon and pay a week's income for an hour of access time. Before you're allowed to sit down at a computer, you fill out several documents, including a police report and an affidavit promising you won't look at any forbidden Web sites. While you're surfing the Net, you're not allowed to leave your station or switch places with other cybercitizens. Every site you browse is recorded by the salon manager, and a complete report is turned over to the authorities if you venture into regions of the Internet the government considers off-limits. Sound like fun? Well, China isn't the only country that's trying to hold back the digital tidal wave. Consider these dispatches from the front:

- In South Korea, the government has been trying to stop its citizens from viewing Web sites run by supporters of North Korea.
- In Germany, raids were conducted on the offices of CompuServe, America Online, and Deutsche Telekom, Germany's largest online service provider. Authorities charged the executives of these companies with giving Germans access to Web sites featuring fascist propaganda and child pornography.

- In Saudi Arabia there is only one Internet service provider. By keeping complete control over access to the Internet, the Saudi government is trying to filter out sites containing information and images not in keeping with the values of the country.
- In Singapore, certain interest groups and political parties are required to obtain an Internet license from the government before they can post information on the World Wide Web. In addition, chat groups sponsored by opposition groups have mysteriously disappeared since the country's restrictive Internet law was passed in August 1997.

And even digitally developed countries face censorship issues:

- In Canada, the Quebec government charged a company with not observing its French language laws on the Internet.
- In the United States, the Communications Decency Act (which would have controlled content and access to information in the digital realm) was struck down by the Supreme Court as unconstitutional.

Each of these cases demonstrates a futile attempt to turn back the next great age of history. As digital and online technology becomes more pervasive on a global scale, existing national and cultural boundaries will grow increasingly irrelevant. Any country that tries to keep the digital genie in its bottle will become more and more isolated in the global economy, and less and less prosperous as a result.

As a global digital marketer, it's important for you to keep abreast of the conditions affecting the development of the digital economy in the countries where you do business. You should think twice about doing business in a country where the government is limiting access to the Internet and other digital communications. Conversely, if a country is actively promoting the use of digital technology, you should put more of your emphasis there, because it is a country that will likely prosper in the coming decade. Consider these positive developments:

- In Sweden, every man, woman, and child has an e-mail address. The national post office established the system and installed public e-mail kiosks across the country. If you want to send someone a message, you use a smart card containing "microstamps." If the recipient doesn't have an Internet account, the post office will print out the letter and deliver it by hand.
- Finland has the world's largest number of Internet domain servers per capita. It also has one of the most sophisticated telephone systems.
- In Thailand, the government has formed the National Information Technology Committee, which sets up Internet depots across the country where people can access e-mail and the World Wide Web for a nominal charge.
- Iceland, an isolated island nation in the North Atlantic, has one of the most active Internet communities in the world.
- In Canada, the average monthly cost to access the Internet is about $20US, the lowest in the world.
- The United States has the largest number of Internet users, and the largest home and business penetration of computers per person.

These examples of prodigital action highlight just a few of the countries where the use of digital and online technology is fostered. This investment in digital and online technology, in business and society at large, will have a positive, long-term impact on the future of these countries. Nations with a computer-literate population, a large installed base of computers, an active online community, and a sophisticated telecommunications system will be the ones most likely to succeed in the first quarter of the 21st century.

THE ADOLESCENCE OF THE DIGITAL AGE

Alexander Graham Bell invented the telephone in 1876. The Wright brothers made their pioneer powered flight in 1903. The first gas-powered automobile was built by Karl Benz in 1895. The television was introduced in the 1920s. Despite the importance of these breakthroughs, their impact on the world was not fully realized until the 1950s and '60s. It took 60 years for telephones to find their way into every home, for commercial airlines to fully develop, and for the automobile to breed suburbia, drive-thru banking, and digital toll expressways. It took 40 years before television gave us the Kennedy-Nixon debate, *Laugh-In*, and the war in Vietnam.

In the same fashion, the true impact of digital technology will not be known for many years. Although electronic digital circuits were developed in the 1960s, the first viable personal computer didn't reach the market until the late 1970s. It was another 15 years before the Internet, and the concept of online computing, began to take hold in the 1990s. In fact, although some of us think we are living in the heyday of the digital age, we are actually going through its early adolescence. It will be at least another decade before the digital age reaches maturity and fully supplants the industrial age.

The digital market is still immature and unformed. Any investment you make in digital and online technology will have more of an impact in the long term than in the immediate future. This might tempt you to put off such an investment and wait for the digital economy to progress further. Such a cautious approach is understandable from a purely financial standpoint, but it's a mistake. If you wait two or three years to begin developing digital capabilities in your business, you'll never catch up. You need to start now and learn with the rest of us. In five years, there will be no shortcuts to the mainstream. You will either be in the mainstream, or you will be a spectator on the sidelines.

It's also important for national governments, and trade blocs such as the European Union, ASEAN, MERCOSUR, or NAFTA, to understand the historical trends in the development of digital economics. The research for this book has shown me that an epochal economic and political story is being played out that few world leaders or policy makers can see. In the next 10 years, we are going to witness the complete transformation of the global economy, and the driving force will be digital technology. Countries that are currently involved in the digital age, and willing to live through its adolescence, are the ones that will experience high growth in the early 21st century. These nations include the Netherlands, Finland, Luxembourg, Norway, Denmark, Switzerland, South Korea, Thailand, Argentina, Canada, the United States, and Australia.

Nations neglecting their digital infrastructure, such as Italy, Portugal, Chile, Taiwan, and Egypt, or actively suppressing the development of online activity, such as Singapore, China, and Saudi Arabia, will suffer economic decline as a result. This prognosis is not readily apparent because digital technology is not yet a significant factor in global economic prosperity. It's still possible for nondigital countries such as China to grow. But, because their growth is based on industrial output, the clock is ticking. Their rising prosperity will be short-lived unless they embrace the digital age.

COMPETITIVE DIGITAL DEMOCRACY

Although the global economic benefits of digital technology are far from being fully realized, the time is coming quickly when they will be the primary force behind a healthy national economy. Digital-age technology will affect every industry and every part of a nation's economy. Digital technology will:

- **Make the entire economy more efficient and productive:** Digital technology will improve the competitiveness of all sectors of the economy, including the agricultural, industrial, service, and public sectors. Productivity will soar, costs will fall, and the competitiveness of digital countries will rise relative to other nondigital countries or trading blocs. Europe, for example, has a sophisticated information system for the trucking industry. The system efficiently routes shipments throughout each of the European Union (EU) countries and brings all of the trucking companies together. The system makes sure trucks in Europe carry much larger loads than elsewhere in the world. This system helps to lower the cost of goods and increase the competitiveness of the EU.

- **Increase innovation and value:** In countries where digital technology is prevalent, the variety and value of traditional products and services will explode. For example, the use of digital technology in textile manufacturing allows for the design and creation of an infinite variety of styles, sizes, and materials. It also allows for just-in-time and made-to-order delivery. In the agricultural sector, digital technology allows for more efficient animal husbandry, higher dairy production, and improved crop yields. As such, countries with digital manufacturing and agricultural capabilities will inevitably export more products, compete more effectively in the global marketplace, and increase their gross domestic product.

- **Foster the development of new digital-age industries:** In addition to improved efficiency and value in traditional sectors of the economy, digital technology will breed an entirely new sector, the digital economy. In this sector, millions of people will be employed to create, process, and distribute digital information. I am not talking about the use of the Internet to promote traditional products and services. I am talking about cyberservices that exist solely in the digital realm. For example, you might develop a company that brings together software manufacturers from around the world. You analyze the market and find gaps in the IT industry. You source programmers in 10 different countries and have them develop specific components of the software. When each component is ready, you bring them all together and market them using e-mail and the World Wide Web. In this digital market, you never leave your office. No couriers are ever used. Everything happens in the digital realm. In another scenario, you develop a private online network containing all of the health-care databases available on the Internet. You create a search engine that speeds up the retrieval of relevant data from more than 500 databases and package it in an easily digested format. You are paid in electronic currency, you work from your farm on the coast of Iceland, and you generate tax revenue for your country.

These examples illustrate the impact of digital technology on a national economy. Digital capabilities not only create a totally new digital economy, they also improve the global competitiveness of a nation's traditional resources, manufacturing, and service sectors. So the question is, Why would any country not want to invest in a digital economy? To arrive at the answer, we need to look at the type of environment required for a thriving, digital economy. Fundamentally, a digital economy requires:

- **Networked cross-communication**: For a digital economy to work, communication must flow easily between each person in the society. People must be able to send digital communications to each other without interference. In other words, the country must have strong laws protecting freedom of expression.

- **Spatial production systems**: In a digital economy, every stage of production happens simultaneously. Workers are involved in many different phases of the process, and work primarily in a team environment.

- **A digital and online infrastructure**: A growing digital economy requires sophisticated telecommunications systems and a high penetration of computers in the home and in the business community. This info-structure depends on a vibrant education system, high levels of literacy, and a digital-savvy population.

- **A small, efficient bureaucracy**: Bureaucracy is anathema to a digital economy. Extensive and onerous regulations block the fast and free exchange of ideas. In a digital economy, the bureaucracy must be small, efficient, and committed to global trade and commerce. It must also be free of corruption and influence peddling.

- **A global perspective**: To have a digital economy, a country must operate effectively in the global arena. Its politics and ethics must align themselves with global community standards. As well, a country must have liberal trade policies, which promote the free exchange of goods and services across its borders.

As you can see, digital prosperity is not possible without a commitment to democracy. In the digital age, people must be free to exchange ideas and to work without unnecessary restrictions. It's no wonder repressive regimes fear the Internet and other digital communications tools. Trying to hold back the digital tide and maintain prosperity within the industrial age model isn't going to work. As the digital-age countries begin to grow more competitive in all sectors of the global economy, the antidigital countries will grow poorer and weaker. Eventually something will have to give. Countries will either adopt digital democracy voluntarily or face becoming so weak that a revolution from within will take place. Either way, financial pressure caused by digital competitiveness will force these countries to change. From where I sit, this is a great thing, and from your perspective as a global digital marketer, being aware of the dictates of digital democracy is crucial. It will help you choose the countries in which to operate. To help you further, let's take a look at a few of the premier digital countries in the world today and analyze why they are so well suited to the digital age.

THE PREMIER DIGITAL COUNTRIES

In the next chapter, I present the Global Digital Marketing Index, an assessment of the world's top 50 digital economies. The top 10 are:

Country	Score
1. The Netherlands	90
2. Luxembourg	88
3. Norway	88
4. Canada	87

5.	Finland	87
6.	United States	87
7.	Denmark	85
8.	Switzerland	85
9.	Australia	84
10.	New Zealand	83

Each of these countries is on the road to digital prosperity. They are also excellent prospects for your global digital marketing program. To varying degrees, they all possess the following conditions:

An Affluent Economic Environment. These countries all have a good standard of living. The high per capita income means their citizens are able to afford computers and Internet access. (They will also be able to afford your goods and services.) Although most of these countries are mature markets, their economies are growing, and they have a low inflation rate: a combination of factors that indicates a stable economic environment. As well, their level of trade is quite high as a percentage of Gross Domestic Product (GDP), indicating a willingness to trade with other countries.

A Stable Political Environment. Each of these countries has a stable, democratic government. Democratic institutions are honored, and even though the government may change hands in an election, the rights of all political parties are protected. These countries also have strong traditions of free speech. Within reasonable bounds, the citizens can speak their minds, or send out e-mail messages, without being persecuted for doing so. In addition, the bureaucracies are becoming more responsive to the needs of the private sector and do not put up excessive and unnecessary regulations that will stand in the way of free trade.

A Vibrant Digital and Online Environment. All of the countries in the top 10 have excellent telecommunications systems. Telephones are ubiquitous, computers are widely used at home and in the workplace, and use of the Internet and other online systems is comparatively high and growing rapidly.

These conditions make the top 10 countries the premier global digital markets. Not surprisingly, all of these countries are mature, industrialized nations. What is surprising, however, is the dominance of small nations, primarily in Europe, such as the Netherlands, Luxembourg, Switzerland, and Denmark. Small countries like these are stellar digital economies because of their size. Each relies heavily on global trade and has developed the infrastructure necessary to facilitate international business. The small, homogenous population can adapt quickly to economic, social, and political trends. They are able to make decisions faster and adapt quickly to global change. In many respects, they mirror the many successful micro-companies that fare so well in the digital age against larger competitors. Like these small companies, small countries can focus better on their specialty and do not labor under unwieldy overhead. It would seem the potential for digital success is probably greater for all small nations, regardless of their current standing on the Global Digital Marketing Index.

In addition to these small countries, you will find larger countries such as Canada, the United States, and Australia on the top 10 list. They are examples of how large, multiethnic countries with complex economies can also prosper in the digital age. Although their situation is much different from that of a country such as Switzerland, they have many features fostering digital affluence. They have powerful, growing economies. They have strong laws protecting freedom of expression. Computers and online services are widely used. They are committed to developing their digital and online infrastructure. As well, their multicultural population, especially in Canada and the United States, gives these countries a unique position in the global community. Comprised of representatives from every corner of the world, Canada and the United States have citizens who can develop trade relationships with any country, no matter what language is spoken or what customs are observed. In this way, the high overhead of countries such as Canada is offset by the multiethnic population.

In summary, the top 10 digital economies are:

- small countries with homogenous populations that rely on global trade and that have made a significant investment in digital and online technology; and
- large countries with multicultural populations that have advanced digital and online capabilities.

All of these countries are committed to democracy, freedom of speech, and efficient bureaucracies, as well as limited trade barriers and regulations.

EMERGING DIGITAL NATIONS

When we look at the countries that rank from 11 to 20 on the Global Digital Marketing Index, similar patterns emerge, but interesting differences are also evident. These countries are:

Country	Score
11. Belgium	82
12. Sweden	81
13. Iceland	80
14. Ireland, Republic of	80
15. United Kingdom	78
16. Singapore	77
17. Austria	77
18. United Arab Emirates	75
19. France	73
20. Japan	73

In this group we again have a predominance of small countries such as Belgium, Iceland, Ireland, and the United Arab Emirates. Each of these countries is also doing relatively well in the digital age because of their low overhead and their reliance on global trade. On this list, there are also a few countries that you might expect to be in the top 10, but they did not make the grade for one reason or another.

Singapore. This small country is heralded as one of the most wired and trade-oriented countries in the world. By all rights, it should be right up there with the Netherlands and Luxembourg. However, the situation in Singapore has one major difference: freedom of expression. For political reasons, the government is trying to stifle the use of the Internet, especially by groups in opposition. For this reason, the future success of Singapore's digital economy is threatened.

France. Although the French have been online for years, using the state-sponsored Minitel system, the country ranks 19th on the Index, far behind countries of much less economic clout. Unfortunately, the digital economy of France is compromised by its bureaucracy and by its uncertain support of the Internet, which is viewed as an English-dominated medium that threatens French culture. France's prospects as a digital economy will be improved when it recognizes its unique opportunity to act as the promoter of the French language on the Net, rather than as its defender. Although there is a subtle distinction between the two outlooks, seeing the Internet as an opportunity rather than as a threat will make all the difference in France.

Japan. As the second largest economy in the world, and one of the largest traders, Japan's position as the 20th digital country comes as a surprise. However, Japan is in an awkward position, primarily because it is "neither fish nor fowl." It is a small country, but its economy is so complex it doesn't adapt quickly. It's a large country economically, but its population is homogenous and inwardly focused. It is a very difficult market to enter, as it has an entrenched bureaucracy favoring Japanese over foreign business. Looking ahead, I would not count Japan out as a digital powerhouse, but the digital age poses some dramatic challenges.

THE MIDDLE KINGDOMS

Of the 50 countries ranked in the Global Digital Marketing Index, it's the Middle Kingdoms (ranked between 21 to 40), that could go either way in the next ten to twenty years. Each of the nations in this group has one or two key flaws that must be addressed if they hope to prosper in the digital age. These deficiencies are:

- **Economic/political instability or uncertainty**: The countries that can be included here are Israel, South Africa, Italy, Thailand, the Philippines, and South Korea. Although they all have the potential for strong industrial-age growth, their political and economic conditions conspire against their status as global digital marketing prospects.

- **Suppression of online freedom**: These are countries with governments, or strong interest groups, that have taken actions to oppose freedom of online expression. They have enacted laws to control access to the Internet, or they have tried to suppress political or cultural content on the Web. These countries include Germany, Saudi Arabia, Taiwan, South Korea, and Malaysia. To succeed in the future, these countries will have to radically change their attitude towards freedom of expression, especially in the digital realm.

- **A lack of investment in telecommunications, computers, and online infrastructure**: For the most part, these countries have low-quality telephone systems, an extremely low penetration of computers, and they have a lower-than-average level of online activity. Countries in this group include Greece, Portugal, Spain, the Czech Republic, Hungary, Mexico, Argentina, Brazil, and Chile.

As a global digital marketer, you should be careful before you enter the Middle Kingdoms. The best strategy is to watch them carefully to see if they address the issues holding back the development of their digital economy.

THE QUESTIONABLE COUNTRIES

The countries that rank from 41 to 50 on the Index make the list because they are currently major trading nations. But their digital economies are anemic or entirely moribund. These questionable countries are:

Country	Score
41. Peru	38
42. Colombia	36
43. Turkey	35
44. Venezuela	32
45. India	29
46. Indonesia	29
47. Pakistan	29
48. Russia	29
49. Egypt	27
50. China	21

Although each of these countries is involved in global trade, they are not good prospects for global digital marketing. They do not have affluent populations or a viable digital and online infrastructure. Countries such as Colombia, Venezuela, Indonesia, Russia, Egypt, and China are rife with corruption and entrenched bureaucracy. China receives the lowest score on the Index because it actively suppresses freedom of speech.

From this analysis, it's apparent a new digital world order is emerging. Rapid changes in the fortunes of nations are on the horizon, and you want to be operating in the right countries. So do your homework. Study the Global Digital Marketing Index closely. It will help you find the right countries for your global digital marketing program. Good luck.

CHAPTER 11

THE GLOBAL DIGITAL MARKETING INDEX

Mercator's epochal service to sailors was the "Mercator projection"... on which the spherical surface of the whole earth was now conveniently presented as a flat rectangle subdivided into a grid by the parallel lines of latitude and longitude. In the late twentieth century, navigators still do more than 90 percent of their work on Mercator's projection.

The Discoverers
Daniel J. Boorstin

Mercator's projection was a tool that gave seafaring explorers a new way to visualize the world. As a global digital marketer, you also need new tools to guide you on your odyssey. That's why I created the Global Digital Marketing Index. It provides an overview of the digital marketing environment in 50 major trading countries. You use the Index to choose the most appropriate target countries for your global digital marketing program.

To develop the Index, I relied on quantitative and qualitative information taken from a number of different sources. From this data, I established 10 categories and a rating system for each category that ranges from zero to five points in increments of 0.5. This means a perfect score for a country would be 50 points, which, for ease of use, has been doubled to 100. (For example, Austria's score from all 10 categories is 38.5 points, which, when doubled, tallies 77.)

When assessing target markets for your global digital marketing program, start with those countries that have a high rating. They are the nations with the most advanced digital economy, and they welcome digital marketers from around the world.

Here is a detailed description as to how each rating is calculated.

1. Economic power: Economic power is determined by a country's Gross Domestic Product (the total reported value of goods and services produced by the country in a given year) divided by the total population. This gives you the GDP per Capita. The higher the GDP per Capita, the greater the economic power of the country, and the more affluent and advanced the market. Source: GDP figures are from *Doing Business Around the World* by Dun & Bradstreet, 1997. Figures quoted are for 1995.

2. Economic growth: This rating is based on the growth rate of the economy in each country. The higher the growth rate, the more opportunity there is for entrepreneurial digital marketers. (The relative scale is based on a range from zero growth to 10 percent growth. Growth of higher than 10 percent was not relevant to any of the countries rated. The growth rate was divided by two to determine the rating. For example, a growth rate of 8 percent would yield a score of 4.) Sources: GDP Growth taken from *Doing Business Around the World*; *The Global Competitiveness Report 1996* by the World Economic Forum; and *The World Outlook 1997*, by the Economist Intelligence Unit.

3. Economic stability: This rating is based on the inflation rate of each country. The higher the rate of inflation, the less stable the economy, and the more difficult it will be to deal with the country because of fluctuations in its currency. High inflation indicates either fiscal mismanagement or runaway growth. In the current global economic environment, I consider an inflation rate of 1 to 2 percent to be stable, while inflation over 8 percent is considered unstable. Sources: *The Global Competitiveness Report 1996; The World Outlook 1997;* and *The State of the World Atlas.*

4. Trading level: This rating is determined by the ratio between the country's GDP and its total level of trade (imports and exports). A high rating indicates the country is open to trade, and is likely to welcome digital marketers for both importing and exporting. Sources: Export figures are taken from *International Financial Statistics,* April 1997 (pages 74-79); the International Monetary Fund Statistics Dept.; *The World Almanac 1997;* and *The Monthly Bulletin of Statistics,* Volume 1, No. 3, March 1997 by the UN. Statistics are for 1996, or are the latest available.

5. Political environment: This rating is determined on a qualitative basis and is of considerable importance to the global digital marketer. I looked at the stability of the government (how long it has been in power and whether there is the possibility of an illegal change in power), the type of goverment (democratic, military dictatorship), the openness to foreign trade and investment, and how well the government and judicial system protect trademark, patents, copyrights, and intellectual property.

6. Freedom of expression: This category is an extremely important indicator in the field of digital marketing. Digital marketing cannot thrive in a country that tries to stifle the free exhange of information. As I contend in this book, no country trying to suppress information will succeed in developing a prosperous digital economy. A high rating indicates an environment that protects freedom of expression, and is therefore conducive to global digital marketing.

7. Bureaucratic index: This rating indicates the level of red tape and number of bureaucratic barriers you will face as a global digital marketer in each country. Countries that have worked to eliminate unnecessary regulations and customs procedures are given a higher rating. Conducting global digital marketing will be relatively easy in these places.

8. Telco infrastructure: The number of telephones in a country indicates its ability to conduct digital business. The more telephones in the country, the greater the ability of the population to use digital and online tools such as the World Wide Web, e-mail, fax-on-demand, worldwide 1-800 numbers, and so on. Look for countries with a high rating in this category. Source: Telecomm rate is the "number of telephone lines per 100 inhabitants, per country" for the year 1994 from *The Global Competitiveness Report 1996*, p. 197.

9. Digital capabilities: This rating is based on the number of computers owned per 100 people in each country. The greater the number of computers, the higher the rating, and the more likely that the population will be using, or preparing to use, digital and online technology for conducting business and personal transactions. Source: Computers per Capita is taken from *The Global Competitiveness Report 1996*, p. 206. (Original source: the *Computer Industry Almanac.*)

10. Online resources: This rating indicates the level of online activity within the country. It was conducted by a company called Nework Wizards (www.nw.com). This survey was done electronically by polling all of the Domain Name Servers on the Internet to yield the number of domain names registered in each country.

World Wide Web Gateways: For each country I have listed three Web sites which are trade and business oriented, and originate from within the source country. Whenever possible, they are sponsored by government or credible business organizations. Updated links for these sites are available at **www.biginc.com**

"Quick List" by Ranking

Country	Rating	Position	Main URL	Page
The Netherlands	90	1	www.hollandtrade.com	138
Luxembourg	88	2	www.cgtd.com.80/global/europe/luxembrg.htm	140
Norway	88	2	www.gulesider.no/eng/	142
Canada	87	4	www.tradenet.ca	144
Finland	87	4	www.memopile.fi	146
United States	87	4	www.uschamber.org	148
Denmark	85	7	www.um.dk	150
Switzerland	85	7	www.firmindex.ch	152
Australia	84	9	www.austrade.gov.au	154
New Zealand	83	10	www.mft.govt.nz	156
Belgium	82	11	www.obcebdbh.be	158
Sweden	81	12	www.mkb.se/engsbc.htm	160
Iceland	80	13	www.icetrade.com	162
Ireland, Republic of	80	13	www.itw.ie	164
United Kingdom	78	15	www.tradeUK.wits.co.uk	166
Singapore	77	16	www.tdb.gov.sg	168
Austria	77	16	www.wk.or.at	170
United Arab Emirates	75	18	www.buydubai.com	172
France	73	19	www.business-in-france.com	174
Japan	73	19	www.jef.or.jp	176
Germany	71	21	www.gwz.de	178
Israel	68	22	www.cbp.gov.il	180
Taiwan	66	23	www.tptaiwan.org.tw	182
South Korea	63	24	www.accesskorea.com	184
Malaysia	62	25	www.cesb.com	186
Italy	61	26	www.informest.it	188
Portugal	61	26	www.guianet.pt	190
Czech Republic	56	28	http://alex.mpo.cz/english/mpo_uk.htm	192
Thailand	56	28	www.thaitrading.com	194
Spain	55	30	www.seker.es/solec/spainbiz	196
Argentina	52	31	www.externa.com.ar	198
South Africa, Republic of	52	31	www.wtc.co.za	200

Country	Rating	Position	Main URL	Page
Hungary	51	33	www.yelloweb.hu	202
Chile	50	34	www.latinworld.com/countries/chile	204
Greece	49	35	http://hepogreektrade.com	206
Poland	46	36	www.cgtd.com/global/europe/poland.htm	208
The Philippines	42	37	www.ahandyguide.com/cat1/p/p426.htm	210
Saudi Arabia	42	38	www.saudi.net	212
Brazil	40	39	www.brazilbiz.com.br/english/	214
Mexico	39	40	www.mexico-trade.com	216
Peru	38	41	www.interperu.com	218
Colombia	36	42	www.latinworld.com/countries/colombia	220
Turkey	35	43	www.turktrade.com.tr	222
Venezuela	32	44	www.trade-venezuela.com	224
India	29	45	www.indiatrade.com	226
Indonesia	29	45	www.cyberdia.com	228
Pakistan	29	45	http://globale.net/~pakistan/liste2.html	230
Russian Federation	29	45	www.dipco.com/busrus/	232
Egypt	27	49	www.tradezone.com/shpncntr.htm	234
China	21	50	www.ccpit.org	236

Alphabetical List

Country	Rating	Position	Main URL	Page
Argentina	52	31	www.externa.com.ar	198
Australia	84	9	www.austrade.gov.au	154
Austria	77	16	www.wk.or.at	170
Belgium	82	11	www.obcebdbh.be	158
Brazil	40	39	www.brazilbiz.com.br/english/	214
Canada	87	4	www.tradenet.ca	144
Chile	50	34	www.latinworld.com/countries/chile	204
China	21	50	www.ccpit.org	236
Colombia	36	42	www.latinworld.com/countries/colombia	220
Czech Republic	56	28	http://alex.mpo.cz/english/mpo_uk.htm	192
Denmark	85	7	www.um.dk	150
Egypt	27	49	www.tradezone.com/shpncntr.htm	234
Finland	87	4	www.memopile.fi	146
France	73	19	www.business-in-france.com	174
Germany	71	21	www.gwz.de	178
Greece	49	35	http://hepogreektrade.com	206
Hungary	51	33	www.yelloweb.hu	202
Iceland	80	13	www.icetrade.com	162
India	29	45	www.indiatrade.com	226
Indonesia	29	45	www.cyberdia.com	228
Ireland, Republic of	80	13	www.itw.ie	164
Israel	68	22	www.cbp.gov.il	180
Italy	61	26	www.informest.it	188
Japan	73	19	www.jef.or.jp	176
Luxembourg	88	2	www.cgtd.com.80/global/europe/luxembrg.htm	140
Malaysia	62	25	www.cesb.com	186
Mexico	39	40	www.mexico-trade.com	216
New Zealand	83	10	www.mft.govt.nz	156
Norway	88	2	www.gulesider.no/eng/	142
Pakistan	29	45	http://globale.net/~pakistan/liste2.html	230
Peru	38	41	www.interperu.com	218
Poland	46	36	www.cgtd.com/global/europe/poland.htm	208

Country	Rating	Position	Main URL	Page
Portugal	61	26	www.guianet.pt	190
Russian Federation	29	45	www.dipco.com/busrus/	232
Saudi Arabia	42	38	www.saudi.net	212
Singapore	77	16	www.tdb.gov.sg	168
South Africa, Republic of	52	31	www.wtc.co.za	200
South Korea	63	24	www.accesskorea.com	184
Spain	55	30	www.seker.es/solec/spainbiz	196
Sweden	81	12	www.mkb.se/engsbc.htm	160
Switzerland	85	7	www.firmindex.ch	152
Taiwan	66	23	www.tptaiwan.org.tw	182
Thailand	56	28	www.thaitrading.com	194
The Netherlands	90	1	www.hollandtrade.com	138
The Philippines	42	37	www.ahandyguide.com/cat1/p/p426.htm	210
Turkey	35	43	www.turktrade.com.tr	222
United Arab Emirates	75	18	www.buydubai.com	172
United Kingdom	78	15	www.tradeUK.wits.co.uk	166
United States	87	4	www.uschamber.org	148
Venezuela	32	44	www.trade-venezuela.com	224

The Netherlands

Index Rating	90
Position	1

Economic Environment

Purchasing Power	4.5
Economic Growth	2.0
Economic Stability	5.0
Trading Level	5.0

Population	14,935,000
Government	Constitutional Monarchy
Language	Dutch
Currency	guilder

Political Environment

Political Conditions	5.0
Freedom of Expression	5.0
Bureaucratic Index	5.0

Economic Indicators

GDP	$330,000,000,000
Per Capita	$22,095.75
GDP Growth	2.5%
Inflation Rate	1.9%
Exports	$195,912,000,000
Imports	$176,420,000,000

Digital & Online Environment

Telco Infrastructure	5.0
Digital Capabilities	3.5
Online Resources	5.0

Capability Indicators

Telecomm	50.87
Computers	0.20
Online Usage	270,521
Person/Host	55.21

World Wide Web Gateways

Netherlands Foreign Trade Agency	www.hollandtrade.com
Holland Business	www.hollandbusiness.nl
Royal Netherlands Embassy - Washington D.C.	www.netherlands-embassy.org

Country Domain   nl

The Netherlands

The Dutch are no strangers to the world of global marketing. During the 17th and 18th centuries, the Netherlands was at the forefront of global trade. Ships sailing from Holland reached around the globe to the East Indies and beyond. Today, in the digital age, the Netherlands has once again become one of the leading centers of international trade and finance.

As a small country, strategically positioned as the gateway to mainland Europe, the Netherlands is the ideal global digital marketing prospect. The government and the populace are pro-business and pro-trade. The logistical and transportation system is unsurpassed. Foreign investment is encouraged. The use of computer and online resources is high and growing quickly. In addition to their native tongue, most Dutch people speak English, along with a multitude of other languages, including German and French. The literacy rate is 98 percent.

On the negative side of the balance sheet, the Netherlands still reels under an extremely high level of taxation (used to fund an exceedingly generous welfare state), and rising unemployment. However, the long-term prospects for the Netherlands are very bright indeed. To supplement its role as a trading nexus, the Netherlands has also developed a burgeoning industrial sector, which can produce an impressive array of advanced, value-added products. In addition, the Netherlands should prosper from the further integration of the European Union.

Recommendation

As Europe becomes a single economic unit, the Netherlands will become even more important as the doorway into this massive market. As a global digital marketer, you should look to the Netherlands as one of your primary opportunities. Any foothold in this country will serve your interests in expanding further into other European states. Start by browsing the excellent Web sites listed.

Luxembourg

Index Rating	88
Position	2

Economic Environment

Purchasing Power	4.5
Economic Growth	2.0
Economic Stability	4.0
Trading Level	5.0

Political Environment

Political Conditions	5.0
Freedom of Expression	4.5
Bureaucratic Index	4.5

Digital & Online Environment

Telco Infrastructure	5.0
Digital Capabilities	4.5
Online Resources	5.0

Population	381,000
Government	Constitutional Monarchy
Language	Letzeburgish, French, German
Currency	franc

Economic Indicators

GDP	$9,200,000,000
Per Capita	$24,146.98
GDP Growth	2.7%
Inflation Rate	1.4%
Exports	$6,400,000,000
Imports	$8,300,000,000

Capability Indicators

Telecomm	55.35
Computers	n/a
Online Usage	3,854
Person/Host	98.86

World Wide Web Gateways

Luxembourg – Business, Industry, Trade	www.cgtd.com.80/global/europe/luxembrg.htm
Gateway to Luxembourg	www.restena.lu
Luxweb Directory to Luxembourg	www.luxweb.lu

Country Domain lu

Luxembourg

Luxembourg is one of the wealthiest and most industrialized countries in the world. It has a high standard of living (10th in the world) and almost no unemployment. Much of its prosperity comes from its high level of trade (it ranks second only to Singapore in the total amount of trade relative to GDP). In addition, Luxembourg has a vibrant online infrastructure (it ranks 14th in the world in the number of domain hosts per person.) For these reasons, Luxembourg scores second on the Index, topped only by the Netherlands.

Luxembourg has two major industries: the iron and steel industry, and the banking and financial services industry. In the past, Luxembourg has been successful in attracting foreign money by enacting favorable tax and banking laws. However, as part of its obligations as a member of the EU, the country may be forced to scale back its unique banking regulations. This rollback could threaten one of the nation's traditional sources of prosperity. To overcome its dependency on the financial sector, the government is promoting Luxembourg as a media and communications mecca. To this end, a number of international organizations have moved their data processing and call centers to the country. This emphasis on multimedia communications is a wise move in the digital age. As the global economy becomes more information based, countries such as Luxembourg, which are investing in telecommunications and digital infrastructure, will reap significant benefits.

Recommendation

Luxembourg should be one of the first countries you consider if you want to venture into the European market. Although small in size, it's a business-oriented country with a growing digital and online economy. As such, opportunities exist to help the country develop its media and communications infrastructure and expertise. During the first decade of the 21st century, Luxembourg will adapt quickly as the digital revolution rolls across the planet. Bookmark Luxembourg.

Norway

Index Rating	**88**
Position	**2**

Economic Environment

Purchasing Power	5.0
Economic Growth	3.5
Economic Stability	5.0
Trading Level	3.0

Political Environment

Political Conditions	5.0
Freedom of Expression	5.0
Bureaucratic Index	3.0

Digital & Online Environment

Telco Infrastructure	5.0
Digital Capabilities	4.5
Online Resources	5.0

Population	4,242,000
Government	Constitutional Monarchy
Language	Norwegian
Currency	krone

Economic Indicators

GDP	$135,000,000,000
Per Capita	$31,824.61
GDP Growth	4.8%
Inflation Rate	1.2%
Exports	$41,746,000,000
Imports	$32,702,000,000

Capability Indicators

Telecomm	55.40
Computers	0.25
Online Usage	171,686
Person/Host	24.71

World Wide Web Gateways

Gulesider Norwegian Search Engine	www.gulesider.no/eng/
Norwegian Trade Council	www.norway.org/trade
Norway Link	www.sn.no/norway

Country Domain   no

Norway

As one of the richest countries in the world (4th), Norway ranks as one of the brightest global digital marketing prospects. Norwegians are the world's most prolific users of cellular and wireless technology, stand fourth in their use of online resources, and are also ardent users of computers. In spite of these digital capabilities, Norway is still primarily a resource-based country. Its foreign trade (18th in the world) comes almost entirely from the export of natural resources and other raw materials.

Although it tries to promote foreign trade and investment, Norway still has in place a wide range of protectionist policies, and the government still accounts for a large share of the Gross Domestic Product (GDP). This timidity is one reason why in 1994 Norway did not follow its Scandinavian neighbors, Finland and Sweden, in joining the European Union. Joining the EU will commit Norway to adopt more open economic measures, and result in a temporary decline in its high level of growth (almost 5 percent). Thus, Norway is caught between protectionism on one side, and the need for a more open market on the other.

Digital marketers entering the country should take into account this ambiguity. Expect to be welcomed, while being forced to pay higher-than-average tariffs.

Recommendation

As a country of fewer than four million people, Norway is a small lucrative market, but an interesting one for the right kind of global digital marketer. The best bets for global digital marketers are products and services that fuel the Norwegian enthusiasm for new digital and online tools, and assist in helping the country shake off its dependency on resource-based revenues.

Canada

Index Rating	87
Position	4

Economic Environment

Purchasing Power	4.0
Economic Growth	3.5
Economic Stability	4.5
Trading Level	4.5

Population	29,000,000
Government	Monarchy (Federal)
Language	English, French
Currency	dollar

Political Environment

Political Conditions	3.5
Freedom of Expression	4.5
Bureaucratic Index	4.0

Economic Indicators

GDP	$640,000,000,000
Per Capita	$22,068.97
GDP Growth	4.6%
Inflation Rate	2.2%
Exports	$201,000,000,000
Imports	$175,000,000,000

Digital & Online Environment

Telco Infrastructure	5.0
Digital Capabilities	5.0
Online Resources	5.0

Capability Indicators

Telecomm	57.54
Computers	0.25
Online Usage	603,325
Person/Host	48.07

World Wide Web Gateways

TradeNet Canada – Trade Resources	www.tradenet.ca
Export Development Corporation	www.edc.ca
Department of Foreign Affairs & Int'l Trade	www.dfait-maeci.gc.ca

Country Domain   ca

Canada

Canada has the seventh-largest market economy in the world, and one of the most vibrant digital economies. A high rate of Internet usage has been fueled by the lowest access rates in the world. (Average monthly access is $20.59US compared to $28.88 in the United States, Germany $74.67, Switzerland $75.12, and Ireland $91.57.) Because of its small domestic market, Canada is also extremely trade oriented. Of the 50 countries rated here, Canada ranks eighth in terms of trade as a percentage of GDP. Canada's digital economy will continue to expand, given its advanced telecommunications infrastructure. As a vast and sparsely populated country, Canada has been compelled to develop a sophisticated telephone system. In addition, the Canadian economy has been growing rapidly during the past five years. This growth has been achieved with low inflation.

However, Canada does have a few negative factors. The country still labors under crushing government debt. Although the federal government and most provinces have lowered their annual budget deficits, interest on debts still consumes an inordinate share of tax revenues. Also, the country's economy has been weakened by uncertainty stemming from the Quebec secessionist movement. The separation of Quebec is still a possibility, and until the rest of the country can find a way to accommodate Quebec into federalism, uncertainty will continue. Canada is one of the few OECD countries that has a formal review process for foreign investment. Although such investment is generally welcome, Canadians are concerned about maintaining their sovereignty. For this reason, be prepared for a marginal amount of bureaucracy when entering the Canadian market.

Recommendation

In spite of a few blemishes, the future of Canada's digital economy is bright. As a prosperous and open country, Canada should be a bookmark on your WWW browser.

Finland

Index Rating	**87**
Position	**4**

Economic Environment

Purchasing Power	5.0
Economic Growth	4.0
Economic Stability	5.0
Trading Level	2.0

Population	4,986,000
Government	Republic
Language	Finnish, Swedish
Currency	markka

Political Environment

Political Conditions	5.0
Freedom of Expression	5.0
Bureaucratic Index	3.5

Economic Indicators

GDP	$121,000,000,000
Per Capita	$24,267.95
GDP Growth	5.0%
Inflation Rate	2.0%
Exports	$29,700,000,000
Imports	$23,200,000,000

Digital & Online Environment

Telco Infrastructure	5.0
Digital Capabilities	4.0
Online Resources	5.0

Capability Indicators

Telecomm	55.11
Computers	0.23
Online Usage	283,526
Person/Host	17.59

World Wide Web Gateways

Business Info Finland	www.memopile.fi
Finnish-American Chamber of Commerce	www.finlandtrade.com
TradePoint Finland Ltd.	www.tradepoint.fi

Country Domain **fi**

Finland

As the country with the most online resources, Finland has one of the most digital economies in the world. With a small, but literate, population, the country has joined its Scandinavian neighbors in their eager adoption of digital and telecommunications capabilities. In fact, Finland has one of the most sophisticated telephone systems in the world.

During the early 1990s, Finland weathered significant economic hardship, but it has emerged as a vibrant, trade-oriented economy. (Finland joined the EU in January 1995.) Looking ahead, the prospects for Finland are excellent as it begins to benefit from its strong commitment to digital technology.

Digital marketers here should find few barriers to trade except for the language and the climate. Foreign investment and trade are welcome, although you can expect a higher than average level of government regulations. Digital marketing is fostered by a number of excellent Finnish Web sites devoted to trade, including the three that are listed.

Recommendation

Although a small market, Finland is one of the best prospects for global digital marketing. Opportunities for export to Finland include computer software, telecommunications equipment, and electronics, in addition to many different kinds of raw materials.

United States

Index Rating 87

Position 4

Economic Environment

Purchasing Power	5.0
Economic Growth	4.0
Economic Stability	4.5
Trading Level	1.5

Political Environment

Political Conditions	5.0
Freedom of Expression	4.5
Bureaucratic Index	4.0

Digital & Online Environment

Telco Infrastructure	5.0
Digital Capabilities	5.0
Online Resources	5.0

Population	249,975,000
Government	Federal Republic
Language	English
Currency	dollar

Economic Indicators

GDP	$7,500,000,000,000
Per Capita	$30,003.00
GDP Growth	2.1%
Inflation Rate	2.8%
Exports	$624,767,000,000
Imports	$817,870,000,000

Capability Indicators

Telecomm	60.17
Computers	0.35
Online Usage	10,000,000
Person/Host	25.00

World Wide Web Gateways

U.S. Chamber of Commerce	www.uschamber.org
Office of the United States Trade Representative	www.ustr.gov/new/index
U.S. Department of Commerce	www.doc.gov/

Country Domain us

United States

The United States has the largest economy and the largest digital economy in the world. It is the birthplace of the Internet, and the home for most major digital companies including Microsoft, IBM, Netscape, and Apple. Its gross domestic product is the highest in the world, and its per capita income is more than $30,000 per person. The United States has the most computers per person, and the largest total number of domain servers. All of these statistics indicate the United States is a prime global digital marketing prospect.

However, the United States can be a hard market to crack. Although its overall level of trade surpasses $1 trillion, this figure represents only about 15 percent of its total GDP. This illustrates the relatively inward focus of the U.S. economy, an understandable situation given the affluence and size of its domestic market. In other words, Americans can get rich selling to other Americans. They do not necessarily need to import or export to be prosperous. Foreign marketers may discover that the U.S. market is hard to penetrate, but the size of the market makes any attempt worth the risk.

The United States has a few regulatory issues that impede its evolvement as a global digital economy. The Helms–Burton law, which punishes foreign companies doing business in Cuba, is an example of the country's attempts to combine geopolitics with trade. As well, the Communications Decency Act (which was struck down as unconstitutional by a Philadelphia court and would have greatly restricted access to, and the content of, the Internet) shows how certain factions in the United States are threatened by the freewheeling nature of cyberspace.

Recommendation

In spite of its tough domestic market, and its attempts to curtail freedom of expression on the Internet, the United States remains the largest and most digital economy in the world. It should be at the top of your list as a global digital marketing prospect.

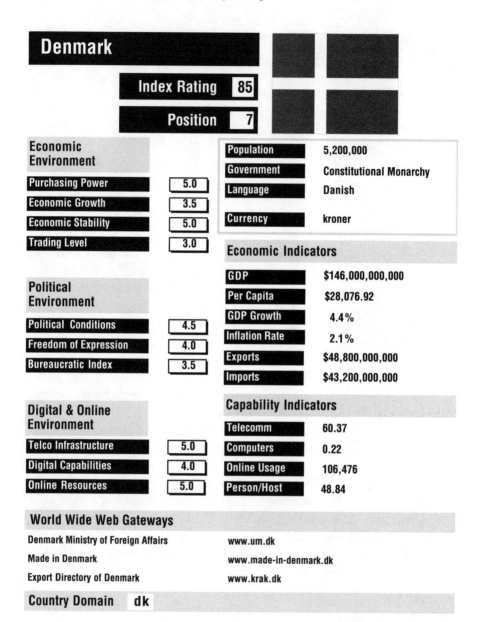

Denmark

Index Rating 85

Position 7

Economic Environment

Purchasing Power	5.0
Economic Growth	3.5
Economic Stability	5.0
Trading Level	3.0

Population	5,200,000
Government	Constitutional Monarchy
Language	Danish
Currency	kroner

Political Environment

Political Conditions	4.5
Freedom of Expression	4.0
Bureaucratic Index	3.5

Economic Indicators

GDP	$146,000,000,000
Per Capita	$28,076.92
GDP Growth	4.4%
Inflation Rate	2.1%
Exports	$48,800,000,000
Imports	$43,200,000,000

Digital & Online Environment

Telco Infrastructure	5.0
Digital Capabilities	4.0
Online Resources	5.0

Capability Indicators

Telecomm	60.37
Computers	0.22
Online Usage	106,476
Person/Host	48.84

World Wide Web Gateways

Denmark Ministry of Foreign Affairs	www.um.dk
Made in Denmark	www.made-in-denmark.dk
Export Directory of Denmark	www.krak.dk

Country Domain dk

Denmark

To trade with Denmark, or not to trade, that is the question Hamlet might have asked himself if he were living in the digital age. But for you, the savvy digital marketer, the answer is an unwavering "yes." The Kingdom of Denmark boasts a highly ind-ustrialized economy, and as a small country, it relies on foreign trade and investment for prosperity (and has considerable room for growth in this area). Denmark was the first Scandinavian country to join the European Union, in 1993, yet it still wishes to maintain strong ties with other trading blocs in North America and Asia. As well, its location makes Denmark the perfect nexus between the EU countries, Scandinavia, and the Baltic states.

Denmark scores very high on the Global Digital Marketing Index for a number of reasons, most notably its advanced and expanding digital and telecommunications infrastructure. The country has more than 60 telephones per 100 people (although many of the public telephones are still analog models), almost one computer for every four people, and a large percentage of Internet users. The Web sites in Denmark devoted to global marketing are helpful in reaching the many Danish companies currently on the Net. If you want to do business here, you will face very few regulatory or cultural restrictions. However, you should be prepared to spend considerable time developing busi-ness relationships. As a homogeneous people, Danes are by nature wary of strangers, although they are friendly and cordial to for-eigners when introduced. For this reason, it is important to work through third parties such as local distributors and existing busi-ness contacts. Contacting prospects directly will most likely fail.

Recommendation

Opportunities for export to Denmark include medical products, pharmaceuticals, textiles, transportation equipment, textiles, and chemicals. In addition, the export or licensing of intellectual property such as software and information services is well protected by strong intellectual property laws.

Switzerland

| Index Rating | 85 |
| Position | 7 |

Economic Environment

Purchasing Power	5.0
Economic Growth	1.5
Economic Stability	5.0
Trading Level	3.0

Political Environment

Political Conditions	5.0
Freedom of Expression	4.5
Bureaucratic Index	4.5

Digital & Online Environment

Telco Infrastructure	5.0
Digital Capabilities	4.0
Online Resources	5.0

Population	6,712,000
Government	Federal Republic
Language	German, French, Italian, Romansh
Currency	franc

Economic Indicators

GDP	$260,000,000,000
Per Capita	$38,736.59
GDP Growth	2.1%
Inflation Rate	1.8%
Exports	$76,196,000,000
Imports	$74,462,000,000

Capability Indicators

Telecomm	59.74
Computers	n/a
Online Usage	129,114
Person/Host	51.99

World Wide Web Gateways

Swiss Firm Index	www.firmindex.ch
Infonautics Directory Switzerland	www.swissdir.ch/
Berne Economic Development Agency	www.gim.net/ch/beda

Country Domain   ch

Switzerland

Switzerland is one of the world's most advanced and industrialized nations. As a sophisticated economy, Switzerland has developed excellent digital and online capabilities, and its telecommunications infrastructure is excellent. Switzerland is also one of the most affluent nations in the world. Its per capita income is second only to that of Japan. Although not a member of the EU, Switzerland has adopted most of the same regulatory and trade requirements. Protectionism and tariffs are low. For these reasons, Switzerland represents an ideal opportunity for the global digital marketer. High-quality goods and services, both traditional and digital, could find a market here, including software, telecommunications equipment, and aircraft and other high-tech products. As well, because Switzerland relies heavily on trade, there are many opportunities to help Swiss companies export their high-quality offerings to the world.

If you are interested in entering the Swiss market, don't be fooled by the country's small size and population. Consisting of three major ethnic groups (German 70%, French 19%, Italian 10%), Switzerland is a diverse multicultural country. Distinct marketing programs will have to be created for each of these segments. However, if you are already marketing to the European Union at large, this should not pose a problem. In fact, Switzerland may be an excellent place to launch a three-language program to be rolled out to the entire EU.

Recommendation

Switzerland is bound to shine in the digital age. Its affluent, sophisticated, and globally conscious people will inevitably make the most of this revolution. For the smart global digital marketer, Switzerland is one place to definitely bookmark on your Internet browser.

Australia

Index Rating	84
Position	9

Economic Environment

Purchasing Power	3.0
Economic Growth	4.0
Economic Stability	4.5
Trading Level	2.5

Population	18,000,000
Government	Monarchy (Federal)
Language	English
Currency	Australian dollar

Political Environment

Political Conditions	5.0
Freedom of Expression	4.5
Bureaucratic Index	4.0

Economic Indicators

GDP	$270,000,000,000
Per Capita	$15,000.00
GDP Growth	3.9%
Inflation Rate	2.1%
Exports	$60,000,000,000
Imports	$75,000,000,000

Digital & Online Environment

Telco Infrastructure	5.0
Digital Capabilities	4.5
Online Resources	5.0

Capability Indicators

Telecomm	49.60
Computers	0.27
Online Usage	514,760
Person/Host	34.97

World Wide Web Gateways

Australia Trade Commission	www.austrade.gov.au
Australian Department of Foreign Affairs	www.dfat.gov.au/
Index of Australian Web Sites	www.sofcom.com.au

Country Domain   au

Australia

If you are looking for a stepping stone into the Asia-Pacific market, Australia may be your best starting point. With a score of 84, Australia is one of the most digitally advanced English-speaking nations in the region. Like Canada, this vast, sparsely populated country has been forced to develop a highly sophisticated telecommunications infrastructure, which bodes well for its digital economy. As a result, almost every house has a telephone, and there is one computer for every fourth person. On a per capita basis, Australians are the largest users of the Internet in the Pacific. In February 1997, there were 3 million Internet users, and 340 Internet Service Providers.

There are a significant number of useful Australian Web sites for global marketers including the Australian Trade Commission and the Australian Department of Foreign Affairs and Trade. If you want to access scores of general-interest sites, I recommend the Index of Australian Web sites. Foreign investment is welcomed here; protectionism and tariffs are relatively low. Although most of its trade is in the Asia-Pacific region (Japan accounts for 22 percent of trade), Australians are looking around the world for new customers and trading partners, especially in Europe.

Recommendation

For global marketers in the northern hemisphere, Australia could be an opportunity to sell seasonal products and services during the off-season. It is also an excellent staging area for the distribution of products into Asia-Pacific countries.

New Zealand

Index Rating	**83**
Position	**10**

Economic Environment

Purchasing Power	3.0
Economic Growth	2.0
Economic Stability	4.5
Trading Level	3.0

Population	3,346,000
Government	Constitutional Monarchy
Language	English, Maori
Currency	dollar

Political Environment

Political Conditions	5.0
Freedom of Expression	5.0
Bureaucratic Index	5.0

Economic Indicators

GDP	$53,000,000,000
Per Capita	$15,839.81
GDP Growth	2.2%
Inflation Rate	2.1%
Exports	$14,442,000,000
Imports	$14,731,000,000

Digital & Online Environment

Telco Infrastructure	5.0
Digital Capabilities	4.0
Online Resources	5.0

Capability Indicators

Telecomm	46.96
Computers	0.23
Online Usage	84,532
Person/Host	39.58

World Wide Web Gateways

NZ Ministry of Foreign Affairs and Trade	www.mft.govt.nz
New Zealand Trade Development Board	www.tradenz.govt.nz
Access to New Zealand Companies	www.accessnz.co.nz

Country Domain   nz

New Zealand

In the 1980s, New Zealand was a bankrupt nation suffering from the long-term effects of protectionism and government over-spending and over-regulation. Through a number of tough measures, New Zealand has now emerged as one of the most stable and open economies in the world. Growth and inflation are steady. Incomes are rising, and unemployment is falling. Foreign investment and foreign products and services are welcome. Few restrictions and regulations stand in the way of an offshore investor or business person. From a digital marketing perspective, New Zealand has a high level of computer and online resources. At publication, there was one domain host for every 40 people—one of the highest ratios in the world. As well, the telecommunications infrastructure is excellent. This means New Zealand presents a good opportunity to global digital marketers.

Although the market is small—just slightly more than 3 million people—there is a need for many business and consumer-related products and services. Interestingly, although New Zealand appears headed in the right direction in regard to digital and online technology, the agricultural sector still accounts for the largest share (28 percent) of GNP. In my opinion, the strength of its agricultural base will benefit New Zealand greatly in the digital age. Nations that neglect this area, and focus totally on knowledge-based industries, may find themselves dependent on foreign supplies of basic necessities. As well, the use of digital technology in agriculture is sure to be a global growth area. New Zealand Web sites dedicated to trade are plentiful and well organized.

Recommendation

There are a number of online databases available to help you find and initiate relationships with New Zealand companies, agents, wholesalers, and exporters. An excellent global digital marketing prospect.

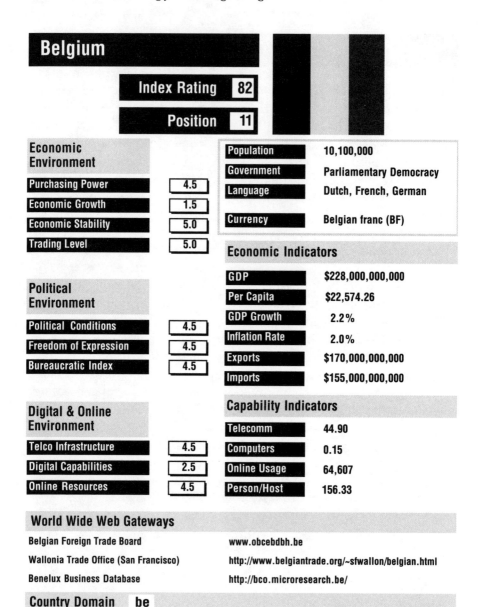

Belgium

Index Rating	82
Position	11

Economic Environment

Purchasing Power	4.5
Economic Growth	1.5
Economic Stability	5.0
Trading Level	5.0

Political Environment

Political Conditions	4.5
Freedom of Expression	4.5
Bureaucratic Index	4.5

Digital & Online Environment

Telco Infrastructure	4.5
Digital Capabilities	2.5
Online Resources	4.5

Population	10,100,000
Government	Parliamentary Democracy
Language	Dutch, French, German
Currency	Belgian franc (BF)

Economic Indicators

GDP	$228,000,000,000
Per Capita	$22,574.26
GDP Growth	2.2%
Inflation Rate	2.0%
Exports	$170,000,000,000
Imports	$155,000,000,000

Capability Indicators

Telecomm	44.90
Computers	0.15
Online Usage	64,607
Person/Host	156.33

World Wide Web Gateways

Belgian Foreign Trade Board	www.obcebdbh.be
Wallonia Trade Office (San Francisco)	http://www.belgiantrade.org/~sfwallon/belgian.html
Benelux Business Database	http://bco.microresearch.be/

Country Domain   be

Belgium

As one of the leading trading nations in the world (9th), Belgium scores high on the Global Digital Marketing Index. Like most European countries, Belgium is behind North American countries in the adoption of digital and online technology, but its openness to trade makes it fertile ground for a digital marketer. Because of its small size and small population (10 million), Belgium has been compelled to look outward for its economic viability. International trade accounts for 70 percent of its Gross Domestic Product, 75 percent of that with its European neighbors. In fact, Belgium exports five times more per capita than Japan.

Marketers looking for a doorway into the European market would be well advised to start in Belgium. Brussels, the capital city, is the capital of the European Union and the headquarters of the North Atlantic Treaty Organization (NATO). Its ethnically diverse demographic profile serves as a microcosm of Europe, making it a perfect test market.

The country is divided into three distinct regions: the northern French region of Flanders, the southern Dutch region of Wallonia, and the capital region of Brussels. The distinct north-south split along ethnic lines has caused considerable division over the years, and marketers entering the country must take into account the differences between French- and Dutch-speaking Belgians. Although these two languages dominate, English is widely used. You'll find this to be the case in the majority of Belgian Web sites.

Recommendation

If you are looking for a starting point in the EU, Belgium is a good bet. The country is pro-trade and pro-business. Look for opportunities in telecommunications, computers, consulting, environmental control systems, plastics, and other high-tech industries. Surf to Belgium.

Sweden

Index Rating	81
Position	12

Economic Environment

Purchasing Power	4.5
Economic Growth	1.5
Economic Stability	4.0
Trading Level	3.5

Political Environment

Political Conditions	4.5
Freedom of Expression	5.0
Bureaucratic Index	3.5

Digital & Online Environment

Telco Infrastructure	5.0
Digital Capabilities	4.0
Online Resources	5.0

Population	8,559,000
Government	Constitutional Monarchy
Language	Swedish
Currency	krona

Economic Indicators

GDP	$196,000,000,000
Per Capita	$22,899.87
GDP Growth	2.2%
Inflation Rate	2.5%
Exports	$79,908,000,000
Imports	$64,438,000,000

Capability Indicators

Telecomm	68.31
Computers	n/a
Online Usage	232,955
Person/Host	36.74

World Wide Web Gateways

Swedish Business Contacts	www.mkb.se/engsbc.htm
Swedish American Chamber of Commerce	www.sacc-usa.org/
Swedish Trade Council	www.swedishtrade.se

Country Domain   se

Sweden

In Sweden, every person has an e-mail address. The Swedish national post office has developed a system that allows Swedes to send letters by e-mail. If the recipient doesn't use the Internet, the post office will print out the message and deliver it by hand. The e-letters are paid for using smart cards containing "microstamps." This kind of proactive digital integration bodes well for the future of the Swedish economy. After a disastrous fling with radical socialism, the country has changed direction. Private business is encouraged and promoted. Public companies are being sold off, and onerous regulations are being withdrawn. However, Sweden still labors under a significant amount of government intervention in the economy. As well, on the global scene, Sweden still has the image of being a socialist country. Changing this misconception will take time. One benefit of Sweden's economic crisis was the devaluation of its currency, the krona. The fall of the krona has made Swedish products and services more competitive in global markets, although it does make imports more expensive. For the global digital marketer, Sweden offers an affluent market for such high-tech products as computers, medical equipment, and electronics. On the World Wide Web, I discovered a score of good sites dedicated to trade, although a number of them were in Swedish only. However, there is no doubt Sweden is a primary digital market. One recent study discovered that more than 90 percent of Swedes were aware of the Net, compared to Spain with only 44 percent awareness.

Recommendation

Looking into the digital future, Sweden looms large. Its current commitment to digital technology will reap great benefits for this country as it emerges as a vibrant, entrepreneurial economy. Bookmark Sweden.

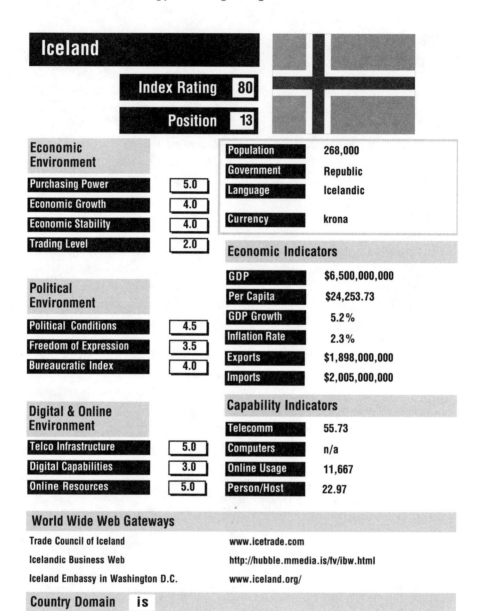

Iceland

Index Rating 80

Position 13

Economic Environment

Purchasing Power	5.0
Economic Growth	4.0
Economic Stability	4.0
Trading Level	2.0

Political Environment

Political Conditions	4.5
Freedom of Expression	3.5
Bureaucratic Index	4.0

Digital & Online Environment

Telco Infrastructure	5.0
Digital Capabilities	3.0
Online Resources	5.0

Population	268,000
Government	Republic
Language	Icelandic
Currency	krona

Economic Indicators

GDP	$6,500,000,000
Per Capita	$24,253.73
GDP Growth	5.2%
Inflation Rate	2.3%
Exports	$1,898,000,000
Imports	$2,005,000,000

Capability Indicators

Telecomm	55.73
Computers	n/a
Online Usage	11,667
Person/Host	22.97

World Wide Web Gateways

Trade Council of Iceland	www.icetrade.com
Icelandic Business Web	http://hubble.mmedia.is/fv/ibw.html
Iceland Embassy in Washington D.C.	www.iceland.org/

Country Domain   is

Iceland

After Norway, Iceland is the most wired country in the world. About the size of Ireland, this island nation stands isolated in the North Atlantic, which is one of the reasons why its inhabitants seek out the rest of the world on the Internet. Unfortunately, Iceland has not yet capitalized economically on its vibrant cyberculture. The country is still heavily reliant on fishing for its trade and foreign exchange revenue. As such, Iceland is vulnerable to fluctuations in the price of commodities, and has experienced rough economic times in the last decade. However, the country meets all of the criteria for a rising digital-age country. It's small, democratic, and wired, and its population is extremely well educated (adult literacy is 100 percent). With these assets, Icelanders have the potential to develop innovative digital and information-based products and services. Their country's geographic isolation will be no impediment.

Unfortunately, Iceland has a few strikes against it from a digital perspective. Its telecommunications system is publicly owned, and its government has imposed a ban on Internet telephony. (This is a technology allowing long-distance telephone calls over the Internet by using a computer. Although the quality is presently lower than regular long-distance calls, there are no additional charges beyond the cost of your Internet connection.) This ban is understandable because it undermines the telephone company's revenue, but it is short-sighted. Iceland should make every effort to encourage the use of the Internet by the public and business. In addition, stringent restrictions are imposed on advertising, and one hopes these will not be extended to the Internet.

Recommendation

For the global digital marketer, Iceland is affluent and well connected. Could be a good market for the right company.

Ireland, Republic of

Index Rating 80
Position 13

Economic Environment

Purchasing Power	3.0
Economic Growth	4.5
Economic Stability	4.0
Trading Level	5.0

Population	3,500,000
Government	Parliamentary Democracy
Language	English, Irish (Gaelic)
Currency	punt (Irish pound)

Economic Indicators

GDP	$53,000,000,000
Per Capita	$15,142.86
GDP Growth	5.7%
Inflation Rate	2.5%
Exports	$44,000,000,000
Imports	$32,000,000,000

Political Environment

Political Conditions	4.5
Freedom of Expression	4.0
Bureaucratic Index	4.0

Capability Indicators

Telecomm	35.00
Computers	0.18
Online Usage	27,059
Person/Host	129.35

Digital & Online Environment

Telco Infrastructure	3.5
Digital Capabilities	3.0
Online Resources	4.5

World Wide Web Gateways

Irish Trade Web	www.itw.ie
Irish Business on the Web (Ireland Online)	www.iol.ie
The Irish Trade Board	http://www.irish-trade.ie/www/bis/itb.html

Country Domain   ie

Ireland, Republic of

With a score of 80, Ireland is one of the premier prospects for global marketing in the digital age. During the past decade, Ireland has experienced higher growth than any other country in the European Union (EU). In 1995, for example, its economy expanded by more than 10 percent. This spectacular growth was fueled by subsidies from the EU and lots of foreign investment, primarily from high-tech manufacturing companies. Ireland is attractive to foreign investors, especially from North America, because it is English speaking and also pro-Europe. As such, a foothold in Ireland is seen as a stepping stone to the European community.

For the digital marketer, Ireland is ideal. Its telecommunications infrastructure has been upgraded thanks to EU subsidies, and there are many well-run Web sites catering to foreign marketers. Although all major foreign investment must be approved by the Central Bank of Ireland, there are few regulations standing in the way of trade. With a small, but sophisticated and increasingly affluent population, Ireland also offers opportunities for exporters. Tariffs run at the EU rate (currently 3.6 percent), and a VAT tax of 21 percent is charged on all imports.

Recommendation

Looking ahead, it is unlikely Ireland can sustain its current level of growth. However, its openness to foreign business, its support of the European Union, and its ongoing investment in communications infrastructure indicate that Ireland will thrive in the digital age.

United Kingdom

Index Rating	78
Position	15

Economic Environment

Purchasing Power	3.5
Economic Growth	3.0
Economic Stability	3.0
Trading Level	2.5

Population	57,411,000
Government	Constitutional Monarchy
Language	English
Currency	pound

Economic Indicators

GDP	$1,024,000,000,000
Per Capita	$17,836.30
GDP Growth	3.8%
Inflation Rate	3.4%
Exports	$242,042,000,000
Imports	$263,719,000,000

Political Environment

Political Conditions	4.5
Freedom of Expression	4.5
Bureaucratic Index	4.5

Digital & Online Environment

Telco Infrastructure	5.0
Digital Capabilities	3.5
Online Resources	5.0

Capability Indicators

Telecomm	48.87
Computers	0.20
Online Usage	591,624
Person/Host	97.04

World Wide Web Gateways

Trade UK	www.tradeUK.wits.co.uk
UK Department of Trade and Industry	www.dti.gov.uk
Price Waterhouse Information Guide	www.tradeuk.com

Country Domain   uk

United Kingdom

Because it is a union of four regions—England, Scotland, Wales, and Northern Ireland—analyzing the United Kingdom as a single unit is not easy. However, the overall statistics are positive. The UK has a strong economy, a thriving private sector, and a commitment to free trade. There is also an excellent balance between high growth and moderate inflation. It is unlikely the Labour Party under Tony Blair will shift the country away from this open-market philosophy. The country is enjoying its renewed prosperity, and it understands the reasons behind it—globalization and free enterprise.

The digital economy is booming in the UK. Online usage is high and growing. The use of computers is one of the highest in the world. The telecommunications system is excellent. All of this bodes well for the economic future of the UK. For global digital marketing, you should have no trouble finding trading partners here. It is an easy place to do business. There are few trade restrictions and few regulatory hurdles.

Recommendation

If you are looking to enter the European market, the UK is a perfect entry point, especially for digital-age entrepreneurs. Areas of growth are in telecommunications, medical and laboratory equipment, and biotechnology. The Web sites listed are all excellent sources of information about trade in the UK. They also offer databases and links to UK companies.

Singapore

Index Rating 77

Position 16

Economic Environment

Purchasing Power	4.5
Economic Growth	5.0
Economic Stability	5.0
Trading Level	5.0

Political Environment

Political Conditions	3.0
Freedom of Expression	0.5
Bureaucratic Index	2.5

Digital & Online Environment

Telco Infrastructure	5.0
Digital Capabilities	3.5
Online Resources	4.5

Population	3,003,000
Government	Republic
Language	Bahasa Malay, English, Chinese, Tamil
Currency	dollar (Singapore)

Economic Indicators

GDP	$66,500,000,000
Per Capita	$22,144.52
GDP Growth	8.4%
Inflation Rate	1.7%
Exports	$119,000,000,000
Imports	$125,000,000,000

Capability Indicators

Telecomm	47.26
Computers	0.18
Online Usage	28,892
Person/Host	103.94

World Wide Web Gateways

Singapore Trade Development Board	www.tdb.gov.sg
Singapore Business Directory	sidgreenbook.com
Singapore Internet Business Directory	http://bizdir.com.sg/

Country Domain sg

Singapore

Singapore should be one the shining stars of the digital age, yet I have given it a "B" average on the Global Digital Marketing Index. Why? Although Singapore is one of the most wired countries in the world (more than 100,000 Internet accounts) and has the third most prosperous economy in South-East Asia, the government is attempting to control access to the Internet. The Singapore authorities have enacted legislation requiring certain groups and political parties to obtain an Internet license before posting information to the Web. This means any group displeasing to the government is denied such a license. As well, the law effectively corrals the three Internet Service Providers in the country. The ISPs are considered "broadcasters" and are responsible for the information their subscribers view on the Web. Most alarmingly, discussion groups hosted by opposition parties have disappeared since the law was enacted in August 1997.

Trying to control content on the Internet is like trying to stop a raging flood with a few sandbags. Extensive attempts to control the Internet will only stifle the growth of Singapore's digital economy. (It is also my belief that satellite and wireless communications will make any attempt to control access to the Internet a fool's game. In the digital age, if people want information, they will find a way to get it.) So once again, we see the interests of a controlling political party in conflict with the freedom of expression embodied in online technology.

Recommendation

Singapore's restrictive Internet policies are unfortunate because, in all other respects, Singapore is a prime example of a digital-age country. It is committed to expanding its digital assets, it encourages trade at every opportunity, and it has an extremely open economy. All of which makes its draconian Internet law even more unfortunate. Watch Singapore closely.

Austria

Index Rating	**77**
Position	**16**

Economic Environment

Purchasing Power	5.0
Economic Growth	1.0
Economic Stability	5.0
Trading Level	2.5

Population	7,712,000
Government	Federal Republic
Language	German
Currency	schilling

Economic Indicators

GDP	$202,800,000,000
Per Capita	$26,296.68
GDP Growth	1.2%
Inflation Rate	1.8%
Exports	$45,200,000,000
Imports	$55,300,000,000

Political Environment

Political Conditions	4.5
Freedom of Expression	5.0
Bureaucratic Index	4.0

Digital & Online Environment

Telco Infrastructure	4.5
Digital Capabilities	2.0
Online Resources	5.0

Capability Indicators

Telecomm	46.51
Computers	0.12
Online Usage	91,938
Person/Host	83.88

World Wide Web Gateways

The Austrian Federal Economic Chamber	www.wk.or.at
Austrian Business Service	www.osiris.co.at/koberger/
Austria Online	www.hello-austria.co.at/ha/

Country Domain   at

Austria

With a per capita income of more than $26,000, Austrians enjoy a high standard of living. The Austrian people are sophisticated, well educated, and open to high-quality products and services from all over the world. Austria joined the European Union in 1995. However, from a global digital marketing perspective, Austria is only a moderately attractive prospect at this time. Although 40 percent of its GDP comes from trade, a majority of it comes from trade with Germany, its neighbor. Germany may be the best starting point for trade with German-speaking countries, followed by the much smaller Austrian market.

Although Austria's digital economy is still in its infancy (there are only 12 computers per 100 persons, compared to 35 per 100 in the United States), its prospects are bright because of its excellent telecommunications infrastructure and its high number of Internet hosts per capita (1 for every 84 people). Digital marketers looking to do business in Austria will face few trade restrictions there, but some of the tariffs are higher than the EU average. Good prospects for exporting to Austria include IT technology, medical and scientific equipment, pharmaceutical products, electronics, and computer hardware products. The number of trade-related Web sites in Austria are few and far between, but the three listed do offer access to thousands of Austrian companies seeking contact with off-shore business partners.

Recommendation

Austria is likely to become increasingly digital in the next few years as a result of a latent demand for computer and online services, which could offer opportunities for the experienced global digital marketer. A good test market if you are interested in entering Germany.

United Arab Emirates

Index Rating : **75**

Position : **18**

Economic Environment

Purchasing Power	4.5
Economic Growth	1.5
Economic Stability	5.0
Trading Level	3.0

Political Environment

Political Conditions	4.5
Freedom of Expression	3.5
Bureaucratic Index	3.5

Digital & Online Environment

Telco Infrastructure	5.0
Digital Capabilities	3.5
Online Resources	3.5

Population	3,000,000
Government	Federation of Emirates
Language	Arabic
Currency	dirham

Economic Indicators

GDP	$70,000,000,000
Per Capita	$23,333.33
GDP Growth	1.7%
Inflation Rate	0%-5 %
Exports	$24,756,000,000
Imports	$19,520,000,000

Capability Indicators

Telecomm	.26
Computers	n/a
Online Usage	1,194
Person/Host	2,512.56

World Wide Web Gateways

Buy Dubai	www.buydubai.com
UAE Business Directory	www.u-net.com/projectp/blitz/home.htm
UAE Online Yellow Pages	www.onlineyellow.com

Country Domain   ae

United Arab Emirates

The United Arab Emirates has the potential to become the digital-age darling of the Arab World. As a small country, flush with oil money, the UAE is in a perfect position to exploit the global digital revolution. Consisting of seven individual emirates run by sheikhs, the UAE is one of the most Westernized Islamic countries. The social code is very relaxed compared to its neighbor, Saudi Arabia. Because of this, the UAE has attracted people from all over the world who want to do business here. A strong banking and financial-services industry has emerged. As well, the UAE is promoting the concept of re-exporting. Under this scenario, the UAE imports products from around the world, adds value to them, and then exports them out again. This concept of re-exporting is one of the ideal business models for the digital age. By focusing on the exchange of goods (or information), the UAE can generate revenues while keeping its overhead light and flexible.

Unfortunately, not all of the conditions in the UAE are conducive to global digital marketing. Stringent restrictions have been put in place to control foreign investment. Only UAE nationals are allowed to own importing and exporting companies, and all other businesses must be 51 percent owned by a UAE national. As well, all off-shore business people must have a sponsor to operate in the country. Authorities are still coming to terms with the impact of the Internet. Serious discussions have been held regarding the need to control access to the Internet and censor content.

Recommendation

Regardless of these shortcomings in the area of the Internet, the UAE has a great opportunity ahead of it. It is one of the only stable, pro-business, and Westernized countries in the Middle East. Digital marketers who want to help a wealthy developing country succeed in the digital age might find a lucrative niche here.

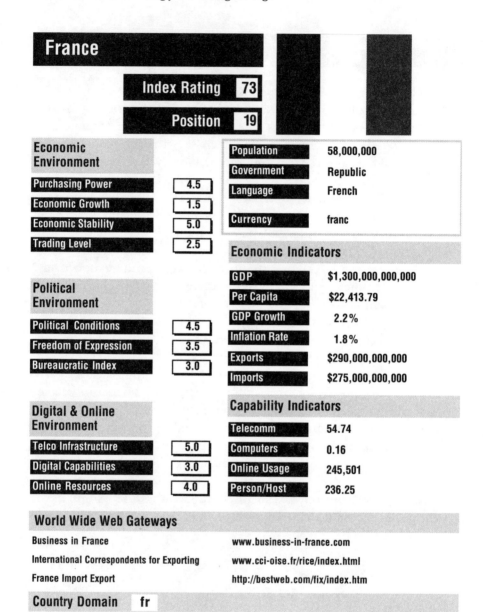

France

Index Rating	73
Position	19

Economic Environment

Purchasing Power	4.5
Economic Growth	1.5
Economic Stability	5.0
Trading Level	2.5

Population	58,000,000
Government	Republic
Language	French
Currency	franc

Economic Indicators

GDP	$1,300,000,000,000
Per Capita	$22,413.79
GDP Growth	2.2%
Inflation Rate	1.8%
Exports	$290,000,000,000
Imports	$275,000,000,000

Political Environment

Political Conditions	4.5
Freedom of Expression	3.5
Bureaucratic Index	3.0

Digital & Online Environment

Telco Infrastructure	5.0
Digital Capabilities	3.0
Online Resources	4.0

Capability Indicators

Telecomm	54.74
Computers	0.16
Online Usage	245,501
Person/Host	236.25

World Wide Web Gateways

Business in France	www.business-in-france.com
International Correspondents for Exporting	www.cci-oise.fr/rice/index.html
France Import Export	http://bestweb.com/fix/index.htm

Country Domain   fr

France

France's development as a member of the worldwide digital and online community has been undermined by its pioneering success in online technology. The country's Minitel system* has been a huge success for many years and came about from a national commitment to online information. However, this existing online infrastructure has made the Internet and the World Wide Web seem unnecessary, and its adoption has been much slower than that of its neighbors. For example, France, with one domain host for every 236 people, lags far behind Germany (112), the United Kingdom (97), and the Netherlands (55). In addition, the dearth of French content has turned off many francophones even though this issue has not had the same impact in Germany and other non-English countries.

As the sixth-largest economy in the world, and a very sophisticated market, France is a difficult country to penetrate. The best bets for exporting to France include chemicals, computer products, medical equipment, entertainment and software products, telecommunications, and other high-tech products and services. When trading in France, expect a higher than usual number of regulations and bureaucracy. Fortunately, as a member of the EU, France's trade policies are in line with the rest of of the continent. However, the French government controls many industries, including tobacco production, telecommunications, rail transportation, and postal services.

Recommendation

For the digital marketer, France represents a challenging, but excellent, prospect. There are many Web sites devoted to trade with France, including the three excellent ones listed. In addition, an account on the Minitel system would be a good idea if you are planning to trade in this country.

* Minitel was started in 1980 by France Telecom, and now has more than 20 million users and 25,000 online services. For more information go to www.minitel.fr

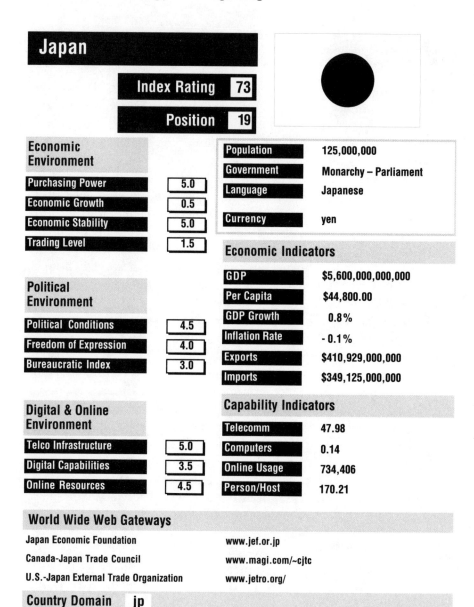

Japan

Index Rating 73
Position 19

Economic Environment

Purchasing Power	5.0
Economic Growth	0.5
Economic Stability	5.0
Trading Level	1.5

Political Environment

Political Conditions	4.5
Freedom of Expression	4.0
Bureaucratic Index	3.0

Digital & Online Environment

Telco Infrastructure	5.0
Digital Capabilities	3.5
Online Resources	4.5

Population	125,000,000
Government	Monarchy – Parliament
Language	Japanese
Currency	yen

Economic Indicators

GDP	$5,600,000,000,000
Per Capita	$44,800.00
GDP Growth	0.8%
Inflation Rate	- 0.1%
Exports	$410,929,000,000
Imports	$349,125,000,000

Capability Indicators

Telecomm	47.98
Computers	0.14
Online Usage	734,406
Person/Host	170.21

World Wide Web Gateways

Japan Economic Foundation	www.jef.or.jp
Canada-Japan Trade Council	www.magi.com/~cjtc
U.S.-Japan External Trade Organization	www.jetro.org/

Country Domain jp

Japan

Although it is the second-largest economy in the world, and the third-largest trading nation, Japan is only a moderately attractive global prospect. Business people who want to tap into the Japanese market will be faced with a number of obstacles, including a tight-knit business community, an entrenched government bureaucracy, a homogeneous culture, and a general mood of overt protectionism. All of these obstacles make it hard to do business in Japan even though the country has very low tariff levels. For these reasons and others, Japan has focused on selling its wares to the world, while protecting itself from outside competition. This has led to huge trade surpluses for many years (meaning it exports much more than it imports), and is part of the reason why the country's economy slowed to almost zero growth levels for most of the 1990s.

To succeed in the long term as a digital global economy, Japan will have to open its doors to business people from around the world, and adopt a more outward focus. However, given its strong culture, this type of global consciousness may take many years. In its favor, Japan has the resources and ability to operate extremely well in the digital marketing environment. Its telecommunications system is very sophisticated, although its proliferation of computers ranks surprisingly low at 15th in the world (behind such countries as Ireland and New Zealand!). Numerous Japanese Web sites devoted to trade are available, most of them in English and Japanese. As has occurred in Germany and France, however, the growth of the Internet in Japan has been slower than average because of the Net's current English/North American bias.

Recommendation

If you're looking to conduct global trade in Japan using digital and online technology, be prepared for a challenge.

Germany

Index Rating	71
Position	21

Economic Environment

Purchasing Power	5.0
Economic Growth	1.5
Economic Stability	5.0
Trading Level	2.0

Political Environment

Political Conditions	4.0
Freedom of Expression	2.5
Bureaucratic Index	3.0

Digital & Online Environment

Telco Infrastructure	5.0
Digital Capabilities	3.0
Online Resources	4.5

Population	81,000,000
Government	Federal Republic
Language	German
Currency	mark

Economic Indicators

GDP	$2,300,000,000,000
Per Capita	$28,395.06
GDP Growth	2.0%
Inflation Rate	1.8%
Exports	$521,018,000,000
Imports	$456,257,000,000

Capability Indicators

Telecomm	48.31
Computers	0.17
Online Usage	721,847
Person/Host	112.21

World Wide Web Gateways

The Baden-Württemberg Agency	www.gwz.de
German Business Net	www.german-business.de
German-American Chamber of Commerce	www.gaccwest.org

Country Domain   de

Germany

As the largest economy in Europe, and the third largest in the world, Germany should have a higher rating than 71 on the Global Digital Marketing Index. However, the nation is still working to integrate East Germany. This consolidation has lowered its percentage of computers per capita and has lessened its trading level as a percentage of GDP. In addition, Germany has taken an aggressive, albeit misguided, approach to online censorship and regulations. America Online, CompuServe, and Deutsche Telekom, Germany's largest online service provider, have all been targeted by authorities. In numerous cases, executives of these companies have been charged with promoting fascism and child pornography on their Web sites. These attempts to control online access have hindered the growth of the industry in Germany, although new laws—which recognize the international scope of the Internet, and protect online providers from unwarranted prosecution—are being formulated. In addition, foreign trade with Germany is not helped by the relatively high level of other business regulations governing health, safety, and the environment. Although these laws are laudable on one score, negotiating them can be difficult for foreign companies entering the country for the first time.

Web sites dedicated to trade with Germany are limited, and the ones I found were not as comprehensive as those in other European countries.

Recommendation

As East Germany is integrated more fully into the fold, and the country's judicial system begins to grasp the cross-national reality of the online world, look for Germany to improve as a global marketing prospect. Its size and economic power make Germany a must-have bookmark on your Web browser.

Israel

Index Rating	**68**
Position	**22**

Economic Environment

Purchasing Power	3.5
Economic Growth	5.0
Economic Stability	1.0
Trading Level	3.5

Political Environment

Political Conditions	2.0
Freedom of Expression	4.0
Bureaucratic Index	4.0

Digital & Online Environment

Telco Infrastructure	4.0
Digital Capabilities	2.5
Online Resources	4.5

Population	5,400,000
Government	Republic
Language	Hebrew
Currency	sheqel

Economic Indicators

GDP	$98,000,000,000
Per Capita	$18,148.15
GDP Growth	6.7%
Inflation Rate	10.0%
Exports	$20,410,000,000
Imports	$29,579,000,000

Capability Indicators

Telecomm	39.44
Computers	0.10
Online Usage	38,494
Person/Host	140.28

World Wide Web Gateways

Israel Ministry of Industry and Trade	www.cbp.gov.il
Interage: Link to Israeli Exporters	www.age.co
Israel Chamber of Commerce	www.chamber.org.il

Country Domain   il

Israel

With a rating of 68, Israel is one of the world's emerging digital economies. The country has a highly skilled workforce and many advanced high-tech companies. Since the collapse of the former Soviet Union, more than 600,000 people have immigrated to Israel, including scientists, engineers, and academics. Therefore, the country is in a good position to export many digital-age products and services to overcome its chronic trade deficits. For this reason, the prime opportunity for digital marketers is to help Israeli companies sell their products/services to the rest of the world. These offerings include software, high-tech equipment of all kinds, chemicals, medical supplies, and high-tech consulting expertise.

For the exporter interested in the Israeli market, the country presents certain challenges. Although the peace process continues, Israel is still in conflict with the Palestinians, and has complex internal problems among various factions within the country. Political instability is a factor that cannot be ignored. However, the nation has several positives on its side. The tele-communications infrastructure is excellent and is being upgraded constantly. Wireless and cellular equipment is widely used in Israel. There are also several excellent Web sites dedicated to helping you develop business relationships with Israeli companies, most of them with searchable databases. Digital marketers entering the country will find few bureaucratic barriers, and a welcome environment for foreign trade and investment.

Recommendation

For U.S. companies, tariffs are of little concern due to the Israel–U.S. Free Trade Agreement. However, tariffs can be extremely high for other nations. For this reason, facilitating Israeli exports is the best opportunity for digital marketers.

Taiwan

Index Rating 66

Position 23

Economic Environment

Purchasing Power	2.5
Economic Growth	5.0
Economic Stability	2.5
Trading Level	4.0

Political Environment

Political Conditions	3.5
Freedom of Expression	3.0
Bureaucratic Index	3.5

Digital & Online Environment

Telco Infrastructure	4.0
Digital Capabilities	1.5
Online Resources	3.5

Population	20,300,000
Government	Republic
Language	Mandarin
Currency	dollar (New Taiwan)

Economic Indicators

GDP	$261,000,000,000
Per Capita	$12,857.14
GDP Growth	6.5%
Inflation Rate	3.7%
Exports	$111,585,000,000
Imports	$103,698,000,000

Capability Indicators

Telecomm	40.00
Computers	0.09
Online Usage	34,650
Person/Host	585.86

World Wide Web Gateways

Taiwan Trade Opportunities	www.tptaiwan.org.tw
Business Taiwan	www.cens.com
Taiwan Business Net	www.twbnet.com.tw

Country Domain   tw

Taiwan

Although Taiwan stands 22nd in the world in purchasing power, it ranks only 27th in digital and online resources. Why? Taiwan's digital economy is being held back by the government, which through the state-run telecommunications company DGT, has effectively monopolized off-island Internet access, driving up access costs and stifling the aspirations of potential ISPs. (For access to a T1 Internet connection, ISPs are being asked to pay more than $40,000 a month.) This outrageous Internet tax is hurting the development of a cyberculture in Taiwan, a situation the government will likely live to regret. This is even more unfortunate because Taiwan has all of the ingredients of an emerging digital nation. As a small country, it relies on trade and has few protectionist policies. The workforce is hard working and affluent. Its growth rate has consistently been in the 6 to 7 percent range per year, and in spite of its public ownership, the telecommunications infrastructure is advanced.

Recommendation

For the global digital marketer, Taiwan offers the opportunity to sell high-value goods such as computer hardware and software, integrated circuits, medical equipment and supplies, aviation equipment, and biotechnology. If the Taiwan government brings down the cost of Internet access, this country may quickly rise in digital stature. Keep your eye on Taiwan in the digital age.

South Korea

Index Rating `63`

Position `24`

Economic Environment

Purchasing Power	`2.5`
Economic Growth	`5.0`
Economic Stability	`2.0`
Trading Level	`3.5`

Political Environment

Political Conditions	`4.0`
Freedom of Expression	`3.5`
Bureaucratic Index	`2.5`

Digital & Online Environment

Telco Infrastructure	`4.0`
Digital Capabilities	`1.0`
Online Resources	`3.5`

Population	42,793,000
Government	Republic
Language	Korean
Currency	won

Economic Indicators

GDP	$380,000,000,000
Per Capita	$8,879.96
GDP Growth	8.4%
Inflation Rate	4.5%
Exports	$129,835,000,000
Imports	$150,212,000,000

Capability Indicators

Telecomm	39.70
Computers	0.07
Online Usage	66,262
Person/Host	645.82

World Wide Web Gateways

Access Korea	www.accesskorea.com
South Korea Business Directory	www.bizkorea.com
Korea Directory	www.oomph.net

Country Domain   kr

South Korea

As this book was being written, South Korea was undergoing a economic crisis precipitated by the collapse of its currency on world markets. The crisis came as a surprise because South Korea had grown quickly to become the 11th-largest economy in the world. This success had been built with hard work, ingenuity, low wages, and an export-driven focus.

How South Korea will recover from this crisis is uncertain, but it must put more emphasis on the development of its digital economy. It ranks only 29th in the world in online resources, and only 7 percent of the population uses computers. However, this low ranking is destined to change. Internet usage (about 36,000 users in late 1997) is growing by 300 percent per year. Not surprisingly, the biggest Internet controversy in South Korea is related to its northern neighbor. Recently, South Korean authorities desperately tried to block access to Web sites sponsored by supporters of the North Korean government. (Of course, these attempts at censorship proved futile.)

Strong protectionism and internal favoritism are two other reasons South Korea's economy has gone into a tailspin. Although tariffs are low, and foreign investment is wanted, an onerous bureaucratic maze awaits any global digital marketer who lands here. In addition, South Korea has lost its low-wage competitive edge. Now that they have tasted affluence, South Koreans are no longer willing to work for rock-bottom wages, and it remains to be seen if the country can produce high-value goods attractive to a global market.

Recommendation

Although South Korea is experiencing the most serious crisis of its postwar history, don't count it out. This industrious country may surprise you by how quickly it can recover. In fact, the devaluation of its currency makes South Korea an even better source of low-cost goods and services. For the fearless digital marketer, opportunities exist here in telecommunications, information services, cable, and marketing services.

Malaysia

Index Rating	62
Position	25

Economic Environment

Purchasing Power	2.0
Economic Growth	5.0
Economic Stability	2.5
Trading Level	4.0

Political Environment

Political Conditions	3.5
Freedom of Expression	3.0
Bureaucratic Index	4.0

Digital & Online Environment

Telco Infrastructure	3.0
Digital Capabilities	0.5
Online Resources	3.5

Population	20,000,000
Government	Constitutional Monarchy
Language	Bahasa Malay
Currency	ringgit

Economic Indicators

GDP	$193,600,000,000
Per Capita	$9,680.00
GDP Growth	9.5%
Inflation Rate	3.7%
Exports	$72,000,000,000
Imports	$72,200,000,000

Capability Indicators

Telecomm	14.69
Computers	0.02
Online Usage	25,200
Person/Host	793.65

World Wide Web Gateways

Cosmic Global Trade Center	www.cesb.com
The Malaysian Business Directory	www.business.com.my/bd/
Malaysia Electronic Publication	asiaep.com/my/

Country Domain   my

Malaysia

As a global digital marketing prospect, Malaysia (score of 62) is light years ahead of its neighbor, Indonesia (score of 29). With a small population of 20 million and a per capita income of almost $10,000, it easily surpasses Indonesia whose population is almost 180 million and per capita income is $925. Like Indonesia, Malaysia has sustained high growth during the past few years, and it is expected to continue. The country has taken many measures to attract foreign investment and global trade. However, it is stifled by a high level of protectionism (tariffs of 15 percent and up), and several nontariff regulatory restrictions on trade. In addition, recent events bring into question the country's commitment to both democracy and free speech, two essential components of a thriving digital economy. In one case, a foreign journalist was sentenced to six months in jail for writing an article displeasing to a ruling magistrate. This episode points to a strong resistance to any criticism or interference by foreigners.

Global digital marketers entering Malaysia should keep in mind the sensitivities of the three ethnic groups—Malays, East Indians, and Chinese. And be prepared to observe certain Muslim laws, which can restrict Western behavior in public, and in marketing promotions. If you want to take the plunge, Malaysia offers the best chances to companies selling high-tech and capital-intensive equipment and expertise: products and services that help the country achieve its goal of becoming an advanced industrialized country.

Recommendation

Malaysia presents a dual image to the world: a country eager to welcome foreign investment and trade, and a country guarded about its political, ethnic, and cultural sovereignty. If you want to do business in Malaysia, you will need to come to terms with this duality.

Italy

Index Rating	61
Position	26

Economic Environment

Purchasing Power	3.5
Economic Growth	1.5
Economic Stability	2.0
Trading Level	2.0

Population	57,662,000
Government	Republic
Language	Italian
Currency	lira

Political Environment

Political Conditions	3.0
Freedom of Expression	4.5
Bureaucratic Index	3.5

Economic Indicators

GDP	$1,010,000,000,000
Per Capita	$17,515.87
GDP Growth	2.2%
Inflation Rate	5.3%
Exports	$231,336,000,000
Imports	$204,062,000,000

Digital & Online Environment

Telco Infrastructure	4.5
Digital Capabilities	2.0
Online Resources	4.0

Capability Indicators

Telecomm	42.94
Computers	0.12
Online Usage	149,595
Person/Host	385.45

World Wide Web Gateways

Informest: Trade Opportunities in Italy	www.informest.it
Italy Manufacturers Business	www.confart.com/lo/
Stelnet Group Network	www.stelnet.com/

Country Domain   it

Italy

Although Italy is the fifth-largest economy in the world, it does not enjoy a high ranking on the Global Digital Marketing Index because of political instability, government corruption, chronic deficits, a poor telecommunications system, and a low level of digital and online capability. In addition, Italy suffers from an internal imbalance that pits the wealthy northern region against the relatively poor and unindustrialized south. This imbalance has led to a northern succession movement which, at present, is more a hypothetical than a real threat.

Although Italy is a member of the European Union, the country is plagued by onerous Customs procedures and a painfully slow bureaucracy. As well, Italy is famous for its labyrinthine legal system, which can tie up business for years. For the digital marketer, expect to find most of your opportunities in the northern region of the country. This is where most of the industry and digital technology is located. I found a handful of good Web sites that cater to the digital marketer; each of them provides databases and links to local business people.

Recommendation

Look for opportunities, but tread cautiously. Opportunities for growth in Italy can be found in electronics, laboratory and scientific instruments, and telecommunications. Not for the neophyte digital marketer.

Portugal

Index Rating **61**

Position **26**

Economic Environment

Purchasing Power	2.0
Economic Growth	2.5
Economic Stability	3.0
Trading Level	3.0

Population	10,525,000
Government	Republic
Language	Portuguese
Currency	escudo

Political Environment

Political Conditions	4.5
Freedom of Expression	4.5
Bureaucratic Index	3.0

Economic Indicators

GDP	$90,000,000,000
Per Capita	$8,551.07
GDP Growth	3.3%
Inflation Rate	3.3%
Exports	$22,621,000,000
Imports	$32,339,000,000

Digital & Online Environment

Telco Infrastructure	3.5
Digital Capabilities	1.0
Online Resources	3.5

Capability Indicators

Telecomm	35.03
Computers	0.06
Online Usage	26,077
Person/Host	403.61

World Wide Web Gateways

Guianet: Portuguese Business on the Net	www.guianet.pt
Cidade Virtual Business Database	www.cidadevirtual.pt
Business Portugal, International Trade	www.portugaloffer.com

Country Domain   pt

Portugal

Following a recession in 1993, Portugal has regained its footing as one of the fastest growing economies in Europe. As a member of the EU, Portugal does 70 percent of its trade with other European countries, although its per capita income lags behind the rest of the EU by about 30 percent. Looking ahead, Portugal has several contradictory conditions that will both help and hinder its development as a digital economy.

The country has one of the youngest populations in Europe, and it is the young who are the first to adopt digital technology. Portugal is also very strict about enforcing intellectual property laws. Heavy fines are the norm. The country also has a low level of protectionism, in line with EU standards. And finally, although Portuguese is the native language, English (the universal language of the Net) is widely understood and used. (There are several good trade-oriented Web sites in both Portuguese and English.)

Working against Portugal's digital future are state ownership of the telecommunications industry (which will keep online access fees artificially high), and high government ownership in many industries. As well, Portugal has the third-lowest level of computer and online resources in the EU, only ahead of Greece and Poland. To grow its economy, the Portuguese government is putting renewed emphasis on infrastructure development. But part of this investment must be made in raising the country's digital assets, or Portugal will experience a significant shock when the digital revolution begins to fundamentally affect the economic fortunes of countries around the world.

Recommendation

For the global digital marketer, Portugal is a limited opportunity at this time. However, as a small country, with the ability to change direction quickly, Portugal is a country to watch closely.

Czech Republic

| Index Rating | 56 |
| Position | 28 |

Economic Environment

Purchasing Power	0.5
Economic Growth	2.0
Economic Stability	1.0
Trading Level	5.0

Political Environment

Political Conditions	4.5
Freedom of Expression	4.0
Bureaucratic Index	4.5

Digital & Online Environment

Telco Infrastructure	2.0
Digital Capabilities	0.5
Online Resources	4.0

Population	10,300,000
Government	Federal Republic
Language	Czech
Currency	koruna

Economic Indicators

GDP	$49,500,000,000
Per Capita	$4,805.83
GDP Growth	2.5%
Inflation Rate	9.1%
Exports	$21,900,000,000
Imports	$26,600,000,000

Capability Indicators

Telecomm	20.89
Computers	0.04
Online Usage	41,164
Person/Host	250.22

World Wide Web Gateways

Ministry of Industry and Trade of Czech Republic	http://alex.mpo.cz/english/mpo_uk.htm
Trade Net Business Information Service	http://tradenet.chipnet.cz/
Trade & Project Financing in the Czech Republic	www.itaiep.doc.gov/

Country Domain   cs

Czech Republic

Since it became an independent country (following the breakup of Czechoslovakia in January 1993), the Czech Republic has emerged as the most open and trade-oriented member of the former Soviet bloc. The country has worked hard to open its markets to foreign traders and investors, but it is struggling in many areas. For example, the country's telecommunications infrastructure is inadequate, although it is being updated. As well, the proliferation of computers and online resources trails well behind its Western European neighbors.

However, there are many opportunities for digital marketers to help the country develop a digital economy as it emerges as a fully industrialized economy. Areas of possibility include telecommunications, medical equipment, computers, food-processing equipment, and infrastructure-related products and services.

As a former communist country, accustomed to controlled markets, the nation needs help developing its financial services industry.

Recommendation

The Czech Republic has many features, especially its commitment to open trade and free markets, which make the country one of the shining developing digital economies. There are a number of helpful Web sites in English devoted to trade to help you inaugurate relationships with Czech entrepreneurs and businesses. It might be your best bet if you wish to enter the Eastern European market.

Thailand

Index Rating	56
Position	28

Economic Environment

Purchasing Power	0.5
Economic Growth	5.0
Economic Stability	1.5
Trading Level	4.5

Population	57,196,000
Government	Monarchy
Language	Thai
Currency	baht

Economic Indicators

GDP	$143,000,000,000
Per Capita	$2,500.17
GDP Growth	8.5%
Inflation Rate	6.0%
Exports	$56,459,000,000
Imports	$70,776,000,000

Political Environment

Political Conditions	4.0
Freedom of Expression	4.0
Bureaucratic Index	4.0

Digital & Online Environment

Telco Infrastructure	1.0
Digital Capabilities	1.5
Online Resources	2.0

Capability Indicators

Telecomm	.04
Computers	n/a
Online Usage	9,245
Person/Host	6,186.70

World Wide Web Gateways

Thai Trading Online	www.thaitrading.com
Thailand Department of Export	www.thaitrade.com
Thailand Business Directories	www.thaiindex.com

Country Domain   th

Thailand

For the past decade, Thailand has been one of the fastest growing economies in the world. In 1997, however, this rampaging growth caught up with Thailand, when its currency, the baht, was drastically devalued on world money markets. Although the Thai government tried to blame the crisis on currency speculators, it was caused primarily by the country's fast-growing foreign debt. (Thailand was forced to ask the IMF for a $17.5-billion bailout.) Whether Thailand will emerge quickly from this economic crisis was unclear as this book went to press. However, my guess is Thailand will weather the storm and emerge stronger than ever. My optimism is based on the fact that Thailand is one of the most entrepreneurial countries in the world. The country is a bastion of free enterprise, especially in Bangkok, where just about any product or service is for sale.

From a digital perspective, Thailand is growing quickly. In a well-publicized story, a member of the royal family, her Royal Highness Princess Maha Chakri Sirindhorn, was hooked up to the Internet at her palace. As well, the government has created a special digital task force to promote the use of the Internet. The National Information Technology Committee has established Internet depots where the general public can use e-mail and the World Wide Web for a nominal fee. In addition, the government has enacted the Internet Protection Act to protect privacy and foster legal use of the medium. These proactive policies aimed at promoting its digital economy should help Thailand overcome its current economic woes.

Recommendation

For the global digital marketer, Thailand is an open book. The Web sites I found were teeming with Thai business people looking for international business partners. If you get involved with Thailand, expect a modest level of protectionism and bureaucratic complexity.

Spain

| Index Rating | 55 |
| Position | 30 |

Economic Environment

Purchasing Power	2.5
Economic Growth	1.5
Economic Stability	2.0
Trading Level	2.5

Political Environment

Political Conditions	4.0
Freedom of Expression	4.5
Bureaucratic Index	2.0

Digital & Online Environment

Telco Infrastructure	3.0
Digital Capabilities	1.5
Online Resources	4.0

Population	38,959,000
Government	Constitutional Monarchy
Language	Spanish
Currency	peseta

Economic Indicators

GDP	$483,000,000,000
Per Capita	$12,397.65
GDP Growth	2.0%
Inflation Rate	4.7%
Exports	$101,999,000,000
Imports	$121,782,000,000

Capability Indicators

Telecomm	37.13
Computers	n/a
Online Usage	110,041
Person/Host	354.04

World Wide Web Gateways

Spain Business Corner	www.seker.es/solec/spainbiz
InterSpain	www.interspain.com
The Real Spain Directory	http://realspain.com

Country Domain   es

Spain

Since joining the EU in 1986, Spain has been forced to open its economy by privatizing state-run companies, and by dropping many restrictive trade policies. However, these measures have not been comprehensive. Many of Spain's trade unions, left-wing politicians, and bureaucrats have resisted globalization and market liberalization. For example, the government still controls a vast conglomerate initiated by Franco called Teneo (or INI). INI owns many large strategic companies involved in aerospace, shipbuilding, and resource development. In addition, Spain has suffered from chronic trade deficits, high wages, and a dormant domestic market. Futhermore, Spain's prospects as a digital economy will not be helped by its protectionist tendencies. At present, Spain has one of the lowest levels of Internet and computer use in the EU. Only about 2 percent of Spaniards use the Internet at work. The telecommunications infrastructure is poor and badly in need of modernization. Spain's lack of a vibrant cyberculture is unfortunate because the country has a good opportunity to host and promote Spanish culture on the Internet. As well, Spain's strong design community has a lot to offer the image-conscious landscape of the World Wide Web.

Regardless of these shortcomings, Spain does have a number of good Web sites devoted to global trade and business development. Each of the ones listed offer online database searches. Also, Spain's tourist industry has been energetic in promoting Spanish travel destinations on the Net.

Recommendation

For the global digital marketer, Spain offers a fascinating prospect, especially if you have already tackled Spanish-speaking countries in Latin America. Areas of possibility in Spain include telecommunications, software, chemicals, and medical equipment.

Argentina

Index Rating 52

Position 31

Economic Environment

Purchasing Power	1.5
Economic Growth	5.0
Economic Stability	3.0
Trading Level	0

Population	34,000,000
Government	Federal Republic
Language	Spanish
Currency	peso $A

Political Environment

Political Conditions	4.0
Freedom of Expression	4.0
Bureaucratic Index	4.0

Economic Indicators

GDP	$279,000,000,000
Per Capita	$8,205.88
GDP Growth	6.5%
Inflation Rate	3.4%
Exports	$20,000,000,000
Imports	$20,000,000,000

Digital & Online Environment

Telco Infrastructure	1.5
Digital Capabilities	0.5
Online Resources	2.5

Capability Indicators

Telecomm	14.14
Computers	0.02
Online Usage	12,688
Person/Host	2,679.70

World Wide Web Gateways

Externa: The Argentina Business Getaway   www.externa.com.ar

Ministry of Economy and Public Works   www.mecon.ar/

Ministry of Foreign Affairs and Int'l Trade   www.ar/

Country Domain   ar

Argentina

Argentina's digital and online environment is still in its infancy, and it suffers from a low penetration of telecommunications and computer technology. For example, as of 1997, there were only 12,500 Web sites in Argentina, and only one telephone for every eight people. These limited digital capabilities are an impediment to digital marketing, but it should not take long for the country to catch up. With its highly literate and educated urban population, plus its new-found business sense, Argentina has the inherent ability to take full advantage of digital technology.

Argentina's economic policies favor digital commerce; there are few restrictions on trade and foreign investment, although the tariff rate is quite high, averaging about 10 percent. The regulatory environment is favorable, with a minimum of red tape facing foreign investors. The peso is pegged at the US dollar (1$A = 1$US), making foreign exchange a simple matter. Although Spanish is the principal language, English, Italian, French, and German are also widely used. The areas of growth include automotive parts, consumer goods, telecommunications, mining, and tourism. Argentina is a member of MERCOSUR, a trading bloc with neighboring Brazil, Paraguay, and Uruguay. Its largest trading partner is Brazil.

Recommendation

After many decades of political and economic turmoil, Argentina is poised to enter the digital age. Under a new business-oriented government, it has emerged as one of the most stable and fast-growing economies in South America. Along with Chile, Argentina is the favored entry point into Latin America.

South Africa, Republic of

Index Rating **52**

Position **31**

Economic Environment

Purchasing Power	1.0
Economic Growth	2.0
Economic Stability	1.0
Trading Level	2.5

Political Environment

Political Conditions	4.0
Freedom of Expression	4.5
Bureaucratic Index	4.5

Digital & Online Environment

Telco Infrastructure	2.0
Digital Capabilities	0.5
Online Resources	4.0

Population	35,282,000
Government	Republic
Language	Afrikaans, English
Currency	rand

Economic Indicators

GDP	$122,000,000,000
Per Capita	$3,457.85
GDP Growth	2.3%
Inflation Rate	8.6%
Exports	$29,330,000,000
Imports	$30,125,000,000

Capability Indicators

Telecomm	9.48
Computers	0.01
Online Usage	99,284
Person/Host	355.36

World Wide Web Gateways

South Africa Business Directory	www.wtc.co.za
South Africa Internet Directory	www.os2.iaccess.za
Guide to South Africa Business	www.interguide.co.za

Country Domain   za

South Africa, Republic of

Since the abolishment of apartheid, South Africa has been making the transition from an isolated economy to an open, global player. This transition has not been easy. When it assumed power, the African National Congress (ANC) was bent on introducing protectionist economic policies. Fortunately, the realities of governing have convinced the ANC of its error, and it now promotes open economic reforms, and foreign investment is welcome in South Africa. However, protectionism is still quite high, and you can expect to pay substantial tariffs on most goods entering the country.

South Africa has a good telecommunications system, and an active number of Internet users, although they are mostly limited to the white population. This situation illustrates the wide gap that still exists between whites and blacks. Before South Africa truly begins to prosper it will have to overcome this inequality in real terms. If not, you can expect racial and social disorder to continue, threatening foreign investments.

Recommendation

At present, South Africa is still experiencing growing pains, and its digital economy is limited in scope. However, the country represents the most advanced and affluent market in Africa. Depending on your product or service, South Africa might be a good bet. There is a demand for machinery, automobiles, mining equipment, cellular technology, and training expertise of all kinds.

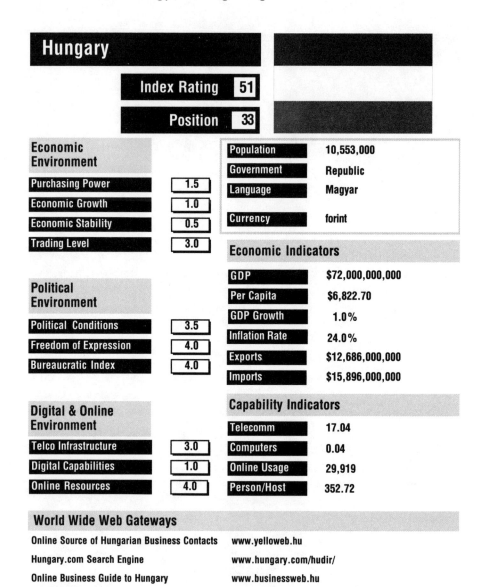

Hungary

| Index Rating | 51 |
| Position | 33 |

Economic Environment

Purchasing Power	1.5
Economic Growth	1.0
Economic Stability	0.5
Trading Level	3.0

Population	10,553,000
Government	Republic
Language	Magyar
Currency	forint

Political Environment

Political Conditions	3.5
Freedom of Expression	4.0
Bureaucratic Index	4.0

Economic Indicators

GDP	$72,000,000,000
Per Capita	$6,822.70
GDP Growth	1.0%
Inflation Rate	24.0%
Exports	$12,686,000,000
Imports	$15,896,000,000

Digital & Online Environment

Telco Infrastructure	3.0
Digital Capabilities	1.0
Online Resources	4.0

Capability Indicators

Telecomm	17.04
Computers	0.04
Online Usage	29,919
Person/Host	352.72

World Wide Web Gateways

Online Source of Hungarian Business Contacts	www.yelloweb.hu
Hungary.com Search Engine	www.hungary.com/hudir/
Online Business Guide to Hungary	www.businessweb.hu

Country Domain   hu

Hungary

With its long-time orientation towards the West, the Republic of Hungary was the best positioned country in the Eastern Bloc following the collapse of the Soviet Empire. In the early 1990s the country was moving quickly towards a capitalist system, but in recent years Hungary has experienced a setback with high inflation and slowing reforms. However, Hungary is extremely open to foreign trade and investment, although it has higher-than-average tariffs and other protectionist policies. Unfortunately, Hungary's development as a digital economy is also hindered by its outdated and government-owned telephone system, and its low number of computers per capita. On a positive note, the Internet community in Hungary is enthusiastic and growing. There are dozens of excellent indigenous Web sites devoted to foreign trade, and the majority of them are in English. Look for continued growth of the Hungarian digital economy well into the next century.

Recommendation

For the digital marketer, Hungary offers a lot of potential, especially in the areas of telecommunications, computers, pharmaceuticals, infrastructure consulting, and other high-value products and services. Once established in Hungary, you will not have to worry about protecting intellectual or tangible property. The country has very strong intellectual property laws and enforces them rigorously. As well, there are few, if any, cases of expropriation or nationalization of foreign-owned assets.

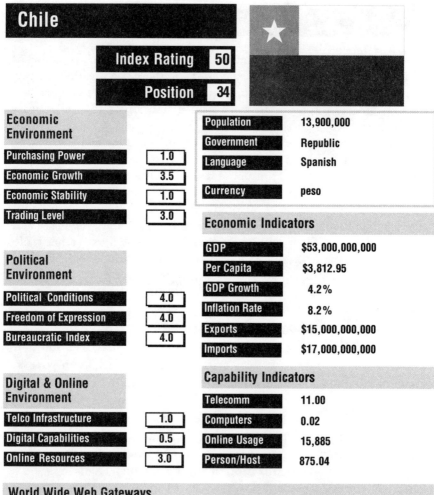

Chile

Index Rating 50

Position 34

Economic Environment

Purchasing Power	1.0
Economic Growth	3.5
Economic Stability	1.0
Trading Level	3.0

Population	13,900,000
Government	Republic
Language	Spanish
Currency	peso

Political Environment

Political Conditions	4.0
Freedom of Expression	4.0
Bureaucratic Index	4.0

Economic Indicators

GDP	$53,000,000,000
Per Capita	$3,812.95
GDP Growth	4.2%
Inflation Rate	8.2%
Exports	$15,000,000,000
Imports	$17,000,000,000

Digital & Online Environment

Telco Infrastructure	1.0
Digital Capabilities	0.5
Online Resources	3.0

Capability Indicators

Telecomm	11.00
Computers	0.02
Online Usage	15,885
Person/Host	875.04

World Wide Web Gateways

Latin America on the Net: Chile	www.latinworld.com/countries/chile
Chile: Directory	www.sunsite.dcc.uchile.cl/chile/chile.html
Trade with Chile Web Site	www.chiletrade.cl/

Country Domain cl

Chile

Since it became a democracy in 1990, Chile has become the global trade darling of Latin America. Its economy has been growing steadily with low inflation under the liberal trade policies of President Eduardo Frei Ruiz-Tagle. As a small isolated country hugging the western coastline of South America, Chile's economic future depends on global trade. To this end, the country has joined two major trading blocs—MERCUSOR and NAFTA, and has worked hard to eliminate many bureaucratic barriers to trade.

As a digital economy, Chile still has a long way to go. The telecommunications and computer infrastructure is top notch in the capital city of Santiago, but outside the city, telephones and computers are rare. With only two computers for every 100 persons, Chileans are still in the process of adopting them. The number of Web servers is also limited, but growing rapidly.

Given its openness to global trade, however, Chile provides digital marketers with an excellent opportunity to sell digital knowledge and expertise in this country, along with computer and telecommunications hardware.

Recommendation

Digital marketers entering Chile will find a warm reception. Import opportunities include aircraft components, chemicals, electronic equipment, medical equipment, and automotive parts and vehicles. Each of the Web sites listed is an excellent gateway into the Chilean digital market.

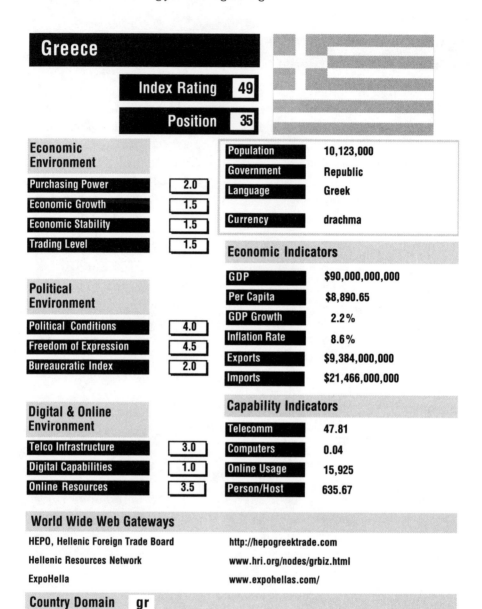

Greece

Index Rating 49

Position 35

Economic Environment

Purchasing Power	2.0
Economic Growth	1.5
Economic Stability	1.5
Trading Level	1.5

Political Environment

Political Conditions	4.0
Freedom of Expression	4.5
Bureaucratic Index	2.0

Digital & Online Environment

Telco Infrastructure	3.0
Digital Capabilities	1.0
Online Resources	3.5

Population	10,123,000
Government	Republic
Language	Greek
Currency	drachma

Economic Indicators

GDP	$90,000,000,000
Per Capita	$8,890.65
GDP Growth	2.2%
Inflation Rate	8.6%
Exports	$9,384,000,000
Imports	$21,466,000,000

Capability Indicators

Telecomm	47.81
Computers	0.04
Online Usage	15,925
Person/Host	635.67

World Wide Web Gateways

HEPO, Hellenic Foreign Trade Board — http://hepogreektrade.com

Hellenic Resources Network — www.hri.org/nodes/grbiz.html

ExpoHella — www.expohellas.com/

Country Domain gr

Greece

During the past decade, Greece has suffered from a number of economic maladies, including high inflation, low growth, budget deficits, and trade deficits. Recent economic and fiscal policies do point to an improved picture, but the country has a long way to go as a digital economy. For example, Greece has a high number of telephones per capita, but the telecommunications system is outdated, and the penetration of computers is one of the lowest in the EU.

Digital marketers entering Greece should expect a high degree of bureaucracy even though the country is a member of the European Union. The Web sites listed provide some access to local business people, although they tend to be commercial in nature. Import prospects to Greece include computer equipment, medical supplies, and pharmaceutical products. Export prospects include chemicals, wine, art, antiques, and specialty foods.

Recommendation

Greece is a small country with a limited digital economy. At present, Greece is not a prime prospect for digital marketers.

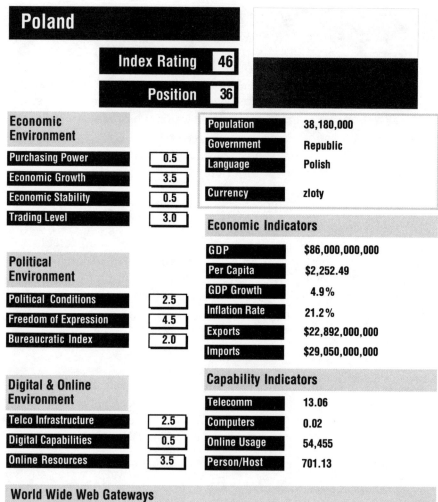

Poland

Index Rating	**46**
Position	**36**

Economic Environment

Purchasing Power	0.5
Economic Growth	3.5
Economic Stability	0.5
Trading Level	3.0

Population	38,180,000
Government	Republic
Language	Polish
Currency	zloty

Political Environment

Political Conditions	2.5
Freedom of Expression	4.5
Bureaucratic Index	2.0

Economic Indicators

GDP	$86,000,000,000
Per Capita	$2,252.49
GDP Growth	4.9%
Inflation Rate	21.2%
Exports	$22,892,000,000
Imports	$29,050,000,000

Digital & Online Environment

Telco Infrastructure	2.5
Digital Capabilities	0.5
Online Resources	3.5

Capability Indicators

Telecomm	13.06
Computers	0.02
Online Usage	54,455
Person/Host	701.13

World Wide Web Gateways

Poland – Trade, Industry & Marketing Information   www.cgtd.com/global/europe/poland.htm

Poland Business Master Page   www.masterpage.com.pl

Poland Business Directory Online   www.polish-bus.com

Country Domain   **pl**

Poland

Since the collapse of the Soviet Empire, Poland has emerged as one of the best markets in Eastern Europe. Growth has been high for several years, and inflation, which still runs around 20 to 30 percent, is under much better control (it ran at about 1,200 percent in 1990). Significant economic reforms have been made, including the privatization of many industries. However, since the election of a Communist government in 1993, many of these reforms have slowed, and a climate of protectionism has prevailed. The government still controls more than half of all industrial production, and the trade unions, which originally opposed the communists, have also pushed for further protection from outside competition.

Poles enjoy extensive freedom of expression. This hard-won freedom has resulted in growing digital and online activity. However, government control of the telecommunications industry will likely keep online access charges high, thereby hindering faster growth in this area. On the Internet, I found a limited number of Polish Web sites dedicated to trade, but they may be helpful in finding Polish trading partners. For the global digital marketer, opportunities exist in the areas of computers, electronics, and chemicals. Looking ahead, it is questionable whether Poland will be able to extricate itself from its protectionist tendencies. Both the communists and the trade unions are generally opposed to an open and liberal market.

Recommendation

Poland will have trouble adapting to the coming digitization of the world economy, and will fall behind in the coming years before it changes its approach and become more pro-free-market. Digital marketers should avoid Poland until these reforms are enacted.

The Philippines

Index Rating	42
Position	37

Economic Environment

Purchasing Power	0.5
Economic Growth	4.0
Economic Stability	1.0
Trading Level	3.0

Population	61,480,000
Government	Republic
Language	Filipino, English
Currency	peso

Political Environment

Political Conditions	4.0
Freedom of Expression	4.0
Bureaucratic Index	1.5

Economic Indicators

GDP	$74,000,000,000
Per Capita	$1,203.64
GDP Growth	5.2%
Inflation Rate	8.1%
Exports	$17,502,000,000
Imports	$28,337,000,000

Digital & Online Environment

Telco Infrastructure	0.5
Digital Capabilities	1.5
Online Resources	1.0

Capability Indicators

Telecomm	1.68
Computers	0.09
Online Usage	3,628
Person/Host	16,945.98

World Wide Web Gateways

HandiLinks to Philippines	www.ahandyguide.com/cat1/p/p426.htm
Philippines Department of Trade and Industry	www.dti.gov.ph
Philippines Business Center	www.mabuhay.com

Country Domain ph

The Philippines

The Philippines is a fast-growing, developing country, and it has made impressive changes to its economy in the past decade. It has liberalized its trade policies and lowered its level of debt. The current regime is market oriented and is committed to further reforms. As well, the government is also working hard to modernize the country's transportation and communications infrastructure. Wireless communications systems are being introduced, and the use of computers and online systems is also growing quickly. Past political problems with communist, Muslim and military rebels have been largely quelled and isolated in the south part of the country. In this light, it is likely the Philippines will enjoy a moderate level of growth.

However, trade protectionism is still high. Huge gaps exist within the country between a large majority of poor, illiterate people, and the well off, technologically advantaged élite who are largely based in Manila. In addition, the piracy of intellectual property and trademarks seems to be endemic. More than 98 percent of software sold in the country is pirated. More ominous, the government and major universities are the largest users of pilfered software. In retail stores, brand-name software is loaded on to new computers as a sales promotion, and pilfered trademarks are routinely added to clothes, beauty/health items, and numerous other products. The disregard for intellectual property rights will be a major impediment to this country's emergence as a viable digital economy. Foreign purveyors of such properties will be little inclined to enter this market with investments and jobs, to the detriment of the local economy.

Recommendation

The Philippines is the Wild West of the Asian economy. There is lots of opportunity, but you have to watch your back. If you enter this market, be prepared for a fight to defend your intellectual property rights. Not a good prospect at this time.

Saudi Arabia

| Index Rating | 42 |
| Position | 38 |

Economic Environment

Purchasing Power	1.5
Economic Growth	1.5
Economic Stability	3.5
Trading Level	3.0

Population	14,870,000
Government	Monarchy
Language	Arabic
Currency	riyal

Political Environment

Political Conditions	4.5
Freedom of Expression	1.0
Bureaucratic Index	3.0

Economic Indicators

GDP	$123,000,000,000
Per Capita	$8,271.69
GDP Growth	2.0%
Inflation Rate	0%-5 %
Exports	$27,829,000,000
Imports	$42,614,000,000

Digital & Online Environment

Telco Infrastructure	2.0
Digital Capabilities	0.5
Online Resources	0.5

Capability Indicators

Telecomm	9.09
Computers	n/a
Online Usage	293
Person/Host	50,750.85

World Wide Web Gateways

Official Saudi Home Page	www.saudi.net
Saudi Online	www.saudi-online.com
ArabNet: Saudi Business	www.arab.net

Country Domain   sa

Saudi Arabia

Oil-rich Saudi Arabia faces a perplexing dilemma in the digital age: Should the country restrict access to the Internet and protect its citizenry from Western ideas and images, or should it open its economy to digital marketing and thereby reap inevitable economic rewards? This question will not be easy for Saudi Arabia to answer. Because this is an orthodox Islamic country, Saudi Arabians and Western visitors are required to observe strict codes of behavior. Women are not allowed to interact with men (except relatives), drive cars, work outside the home, or wear body-revealing clothing. Serious penalties are meted out for violations. In this environment, it's no wonder Saudi Arabia does not yet have an Internet Service Provider. At the time of writing, the Saudi government was planning to grant a license to one ISP, which will be required to filter out all undesirable Web sites. Usage will be monitored to detect online malfeasance.

In my opinion, this type of control will hinder the development of the Saudi economy. With use of few computers, and severely restricted access to the Internet, Saudi Arabia will be hard put to diversify its economy and reduce its reliance on oil revenues. The dilemma faced by Saudi Arabia illustrates perfectly the true impact of the digital and online revolution. Countries are forced to choose between increased prosperity or protection of their culture. In this case, Saudi Arabia may choose to protect its culture, which is its right. However, cultural sovereignty will not come without an economic cost.

Recommendation

For the digital global marketer, Saudi Arabia does offer some opportunities, especially in the area of consulting. If you wish to work in Saudi Arabia, the Web offers some contacts. Check out the listed sites.

Brazil

Index Rating 40

Position 39

Economic Environment

Purchasing Power	1.0
Economic Growth	4.0
Economic Stability	0.5
Trading Level	1.0

Political Environment

Political Conditions	4.0
Freedom of Expression	4.0
Bureaucratic Index	2.5

Digital & Online Environment

Telco Infrastructure	0.5
Digital Capabilities	0
Online Resources	2.5

Population	155,000,000
Government	Federal Republic
Language	Portuguese
Currency	real

Economic Indicators

GDP	$550,000,000,000
Per Capita	$3,548.39
GDP Growth	5.7%
Inflation Rate	19.0%
Exports	$47,000,000,000
Imports	$56,000,000,000

Capability Indicators

Telecomm	07.38
Computers	0.01
Online Usage	77,148
Person/Host	2,009.13

World Wide Web Gateways

Brazilian Business Connection	www.brazilbiz.com.br/english/
Brazil Business Development Program	www.bbd.com.br/
The Brazilian Trade Center	www.nogalink.com/

Country Domain   br

Brazil

Although Brazil is by far the largest economy in Latin America, it scores low on the Global Digital Marketing Index because of its volatile economy, high bureaucratic complexity, and inadequate telecommunications and digital infrastructure. Although inflation has fallen from its astronomical levels of a few years ago, it is still high compared to more stable countries (about 20 percent). Foreign business people entering Brazil should be prepared to face many complications and regulations, and much red tape. In addition, Brazil's digital economy is hindered by its high level of poverty, and by its small number of computers (less than one computer per 100 people). A major concern is the protection of intellectual property rights. Historically, the rights of many global marketers have been violated and Brazilian judicial authorities provided little help.

However, Brazil does offer some promise of better things to come for the global digital marketer. Although the number of quality Web sites in Brazil is limited, we did find a handful that are useful if you want to initiate a business relationship in the major cities of Rio de Janeiro, Sao Paulo, and Brasilia. Areas of opportunity in Brazil include the following sectors: electronics, media equipment and supplies, organic chemicals, security and safety equipment, pollution control devices, telecommunications products, information technology, and pharmaceuticals. From my personal experience, Brazilians are gregarious and friendly, and interested in foreign places and people.

Brazil is also hindered in its development as a digital economy because of its language. With Portuguese as its official language, Brazil is linguistically isolated from its Latin American neighbors, and from the Net community.

Recommendation

In Brazil, you cannot be in a hurry to make a sale. Considerable time must be spent developing a personal relationship before moving on to business. Because of its size and potential, Brazil is an exciting national market. But exercise caution.

Mexico

Index Rating	39
Position	40

Economic Environment

Purchasing Power	1.0
Economic Growth	3.5
Economic Stability	0.5
Trading Level	1.5

Political Environment

Political Conditions	2.5
Freedom of Expression	3.5
Bureaucratic Index	2.0

Digital & Online Environment

Telco Infrastructure	2.0
Digital Capabilities	0.5
Online Resources	2.5

Population	92,000,000
Government	Federal Republic
Language	Spanish
Currency	peso

Economic Indicators

GDP	$377,000,000,000
Per Capita	$4,097.83
GDP Growth	4.5%
Inflation Rate	35.0%
Exports	$48,430,000,000
Imports	$46,887,000,000

Capability Indicators

Telecomm	9.25
Computers	0.02
Online Usage	29,840
Person/Host	3,083.11

World Wide Web Gateways

Mexico Information Center	www.mexico-trade.com
Mexico Business Home Page	www.nafta.net/mexbiz
Mexico Business and Trade	www.mexicobusinessandtrade.com

Country Domain   mx

Mexico

Since the collapse of the Mexican peso in December 1994, the country has been struggling to regain its footing as a fast-growing, developing country. In all categories of the Global Digital Marketing Index, Mexico lags far behind its two NAFTA partners, Canada and the United States. With a per capita income of just over $4,000, most Mexicans still live in poverty. The country's inflation rate is very high, hovering around 35 percent. The political environment is uncertain, with a dangerous degree of corruption practiced by both elected and bureaucratic officials. The telecommunications infrastructure is outmoded, inconsistent, and expensive. Only a small percentage of the population uses computers, and there is only a modest level of online activity. In its favor, Mexico has a strong trade surplus as the devalued peso has lowered the cost of Mexican exports around the world. However, for the global digital marketer, the devalued peso also makes foreign goods relatively much more expensive for Mexicans. Fortunately, Mexico's membership in NAFTA has forced the country to undertake a number of important trade reforms. As well, Mexico has negotiated bilateral trade agreements with numerous non-NAFTA countries.

As the southern neighbor to the United States, the world's leading economy, Mexico can also be expected to put more emphasis on the development of its digital and online capabilities.

Recommendation

Looking ahead, expect Mexico to continue its strong growth, but it might be interrupted regularly by further political and economic hiccups. On the World Wide Web, there are a handful of good Web sites that offer marketers a digital doorway into Mexico. Opportunities for export to Mexico exist for environmental control systems, chemical production equipment, electronic components, and telecommunications systems.

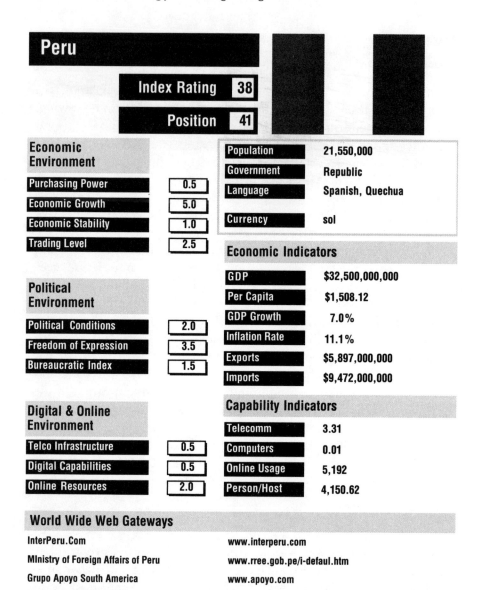

Peru

Index Rating	38
Position	41

Economic Environment

Purchasing Power	0.5
Economic Growth	5.0
Economic Stability	1.0
Trading Level	2.5

Population	21,550,000
Government	Republic
Language	Spanish, Quechua
Currency	sol

Political Environment

Political Conditions	2.0
Freedom of Expression	3.5
Bureaucratic Index	1.5

Economic Indicators

GDP	$32,500,000,000
Per Capita	$1,508.12
GDP Growth	7.0%
Inflation Rate	11.1%
Exports	$5,897,000,000
Imports	$9,472,000,000

Digital & Online Environment

Telco Infrastructure	0.5
Digital Capabilities	0.5
Online Resources	2.0

Capability Indicators

Telecomm	3.31
Computers	0.01
Online Usage	5,192
Person/Host	4,150.62

World Wide Web Gateways

InterPeru.Com	www.interperu.com
MInistry of Foreign Affairs of Peru	www.rree.gob.pe/i-defaul.htm
Grupo Apoyo South America	www.apoyo.com

Country Domain   pe

Peru

During the 1980s Peru was a bankrupt nation. With soaring debts and rampant inflation, Peru was cut off from the International Monetary Fund (IMF). With the election of the Fujimori government in 1990, the country set off on the road to recovery. Inflation has been tamed, and its debts are coming under control. Today, Peru stands at a crossroad. It will either enter the digital age through the promotion of digital and online capabilities, or it will lapse into its former delinquent state. On the plus side, Peru continues to maintain solid growth (the fastest in the world in 1994), while holding the reins on inflation (although still at an above average rate of 10 percent).

On the negative side, the Peruvian government continues to wage war with indigenous rebel groups. As well, the level of black market activity is extremely high, with little effort made to enforce international copyrights and trademarks. For example, pirated software accounts for 80 percent of the market in Peru. Books are routinely copied and sold. Peru is therefore a risky country for global digital marketers, especially for those hawking intellectual properties. Greater success may be realized from helping the country overcome its reliance on fishing as its major foreign trade. Consultants in the areas of information technology may do well in Peru, as long as they can speak Spanish.

Recommendation

On the Internet, Peru is well represented, indicating an effort to promote online activity. I found a number of interesting sites that promote trade. However, most of this activity is limited to the major cities on the coast such as the capital of Lima. The population living inland is not part of the modern economy, and it is unlikely this segment of the population will become online users in the near future. At present, Peru is not a good global digital marketing prospect.

Colombia

| Index Rating | 36 |
| Position | 42 |

Economic Environment

Purchasing Power	1.5
Economic Growth	4.5
Economic Stability	0.5
Trading Level	0.5

Population	34,300,000
Government	Republic
Language	Spanish
Currency	peso

Political Environment

Political Conditions	1.0
Freedom of Expression	3.5
Bureaucratic Index	2.0

Economic Indicators

GDP	$60,000,000,000
Per Capita	$1,749.27
GDP Growth	6.5%
Inflation Rate	21.0%
Exports	$10,500,000,000
Imports	$13,700,000,000

Digital & Online Environment

Telco Infrastructure	2.0
Digital Capabilities	0.5
Online Resources	2.0

Capability Indicators

Telecomm	9.68
Computers	0.02
Online Usage	9,054
Person/Host	3,788.38

World Wide Web Gateways

Latin America on the Net: Colombia	www.latinworld.com/countries/colombia
Colombia Network	www.latinet.com/colnet.htm
Global Cham. of Comm: Business in Colombia	www.gcc.net/commerce/america/colombia.htm

Country Domain   CO

Colombia

In recent years, Colombia has made serious attempts to improve its image on the world stage. The government has tried to clean up the corruption, organized crime, and violence that have plagued this Latin American country for decades. Unfortunately, these well-intentioned efforts have had limited success. The drug trade continues unabated. Politicians are still susceptible to corruption. Leftist guerillas still control rural areas, and the level of violence remains high (the rate of violent death in Colombia is eight times higher than in the United States). In addition, inflation remains very high due to a massive influx of contraband drug dollars.

As a global digital marketing prospect, Colombia is an extremely risky place to conduct business. Foreign business people are routinely kidnapped and held for ransom. Often the wrong people are abducted. In fact, the problem is so bad, most foreign nationals working in Colombia have "kidnap and ransom" insurance. In the event you are kidnapped, the insurance company will handle the entire process, which includes negotiating with the captors, paying the ransom, and reimbursing you for any income lost during your captivity. It is probably a good idea to avoid Colombia altogether or conduct all of your business over the Internet from the safety of your own office.

Recommendation

Until Colombia is successful in controlling its level of organized crime, this country is an extemely poor prospect for global digital marketing.

Turkey

Index Rating	35
Position	43

Economic Environment

Purchasing Power	0.5
Economic Growth	0.5
Economic Stability	0.5
Trading Level	2.0

Political Environment

Political Conditions	3.0
Freedom of Expression	3.5
Bureaucratic Index	3.0

Digital & Online Environment

Telco Infrastructure	2.0
Digital Capabilities	0.5
Online Resources	2.0

Population	62,000,000
Government	Republic
Language	Turkish
Currency	lira

Economic Indicators

GDP	$180,000,000,000
Per Capita	$2,903.23
GDP Growth	- 6.0%
Inflation Rate	93.6%
Exports	$21,600,000,000
Imports	$35,710,000,000

Capability Indicators

Telecomm	20.10
Computers	0.01
Online Usage	13,194
Person/Host	4,699.11

World Wide Web Gateways

TurkTrade – Turkey Trade Center	www.turktrade.com.tr
Discover Turkey: Business and Economy	www.turkishnews.com/DiscoverTurkey/economy/
Turkey Foreign Trade Center	www.turkex.com

Country Domain   tr

Turkey

Turkey has always stood as a bridge between Europe and Asia, and at the end of the 1990s, Turkey is once again at a crossroad. Turkey can continue on its present course and eventually become a member of the European Union, or it can move towards becoming an Islamic state. This choice is best illustrated by its current government, a coalition between the Islamic Welfare Party and the secular True Path Party. The emergence of the Islamic party as a viable force in Turkish politics has raised questions about Turkey's future as a Westernized economy. Should the Welfare Party assume a majority in the government, the country will likely move closer to other Islamic countries and away from the EU. Until this question is answered, Turkey's development as a digital economy will also stagnate. Although it has a dependable telephone system, the rate of computer use is extremely low.

Of 50 countries ranked here, Turkey is 39th in online resources. I did, however, find two Web sites that promote Turkish business and trade. They could be helpful if you are interested in exporting to Turkey. Opportunities exist in the areas of telecommunications, electric power systems, software and electronics. To tap into this market, the best strategy is to enlist the help of a local agent or wholesaler, who will help you navigate this complex country.

Recommendation

Until the direction of the country is settled, be careful about significant investments in Turkey.

Venezuela

Index Rating	32
Position	44

Economic Environment

Purchasing Power	0.5
Economic Growth	1.5
Economic Stability	0.5
Trading Level	1.0

Population	19,735,000
Government	Federal Republic
Language	Spanish
Currency	bolivar

Political Environment

Political Conditions	2.5
Freedom of Expression	3.0
Bureaucratic Index	3.0

Economic Indicators

GDP	$56,000,000,000
Per Capita	$2,837.60
GDP Growth	2.2%
Inflation Rate	59.9%
Exports	$18,300,000,000
Imports	$11,600,000,000

Digital & Online Environment

Telco Infrastructure	2.0
Digital Capabilities	0.5
Online Resources	1.5

Capability Indicators

Telecomm	10.92
Computers	0.02
Online Usage	2,417
Person/Host	8,165.08

World Wide Web Gateways

Trade Venezuela	www.trade-venezuela.com
The Venezuelan Trade Directory	www.ddex.com.ve
Embassy of Venezuela, Washington D.C.	http://venezuela.mit.edu/embassy/

Country Domain   ve

Venezuela

Over the course of the 1990s, Venezuela has experienced severe economic shocks, including a virtual collapse of the banking system, a devaluation of its currency, and a high rate of inflation. In response, the government has imposed price and foreign exchange controls, and has taken other measures that stifle the free market. Unfortunately, the trend towards further intervention is continuing. This situation has made Venezuela a risky place to do business, and the unstable economy has scared away foreign investors. As a digital economy, Venezuela is backward, and its culture suggests it will remain that way. The Venezeulan culture is hierarchical and authoritarian. It is one of the most male-oriented countries in Latin America, a region known for its machismo. These characteristics do not foster the evolution of an open, networked society. Whatever the outcome, the process will be interesting.

If you do decide to venture into Venezuela, be prepared. The country is an expensive place to do business. Nepotism is the rule, and foreign business people must take a back seat to local loyalties. Although Venezuela has signed most international treaties governing the protection of trademarks and intellectual property, enforcement is anemic at best. In terms of communications, the telephone system is quite extensive, but it can be unreliable, and still needs to be upgraded to a digital system.

Recommendation

Watch Venezuela closely in coming years. An interesting drama will be played out as a traditional, male-oriented, and top-down culture interfaces with the digital revolution.

India

Index Rating	29
Position	45

Economic Environment

Purchasing Power	0.5
Economic Growth	3.5
Economic Stability	1.0
Trading Level	1.0

Population	843,931,000
Government	Republic
Language	Hindi, English
Currency	rupee

Political Environment

Political Conditions	3.0
Freedom of Expression	3.5
Bureaucratic Index	1.5

Economic Indicators

GDP	$300,000,000,000
Per Capita	$355.48
GDP Growth	5.0%
Inflation Rate	10.2%
Exports	$33,025,000,000
Imports	$37,177,000,000

Digital & Online Environment

Telco Infrastructure	0.5
Digital Capabilities	0
Online Resources	0

Capability Indicators

Telecomm	1.07
Computers	n/a
Online Usage	3,138
Person/Host	268,939.13

World Wide Web Gateways

India Trade	www.indiatrade.com
India Online	www.indiaonline.com
Trade Opportunities in India	www.bankofindia.com/boi_trade.html

Country Domain   in

India

India has been dubbed as the one of the fastest growing, emerging markets in the world. Its digital economy, however, still has a long way to go before it even remotely approaches Western levels. In the early 1990s, India suffered through a difficult economic crisis which resulted partly from its protectionist, antitrade policies. Since that time, the nation has endeavored to open up to international trade and investment. These measures have worked, but it remains to be seen if the trend toward globalization will continue. Antiforeign bias is common in India, and the protection of foreign property, both tangible and intellectual, is still difficult.

India represents a vast, untapped market (that is growing rapidly) of almost 900 million people. There is a middle class of more than 200 million, probably the largest in the world. India may make the leap directly from a first wave economy (based on agriculture) to a third wave economy through the development of wireless and satellite-based communications systems, rather than a traditional "wire" infrastructure. As well, the widespread use of English in India means the country will be able to merge more easily with the (predominantly) English online universe. However, India will be hindered in its digital aspirations by widespread poverty, rampant population growth, and its relatively inward-focused economy.

Given the country's political complexity, and multiethinic composition, the future remains uncertain.

Recommendation

Although India is one of the more complex and challenging markets in which to work, it deserves attention for its size and potential.

Indonesia

Index Rating	**29**
Position	**45**

Economic Environment

Purchasing Power	0.5
Economic Growth	5.0
Economic Stability	1.0
Trading Level	2.5

Political Environment

Political Conditions	2.0
Freedom of Expression	1.0
Bureaucratic Index	1.0

Digital & Online Environment

Telco Infrastructure	0.5
Digital Capabilities	0
Online Resources	1.0

Population	179,300,000
Government	Republic
Language	Bahasa Indonesia
Currency	rupiah

Economic Indicators

GDP	$166,000,000,000
Per Capita	$925.82
GDP Growth	7.3%
Inflation Rate	9.4%
Exports	$45,417,000,000
Imports	$40,629,000,000

Capability Indicators

Telecomm	1.33
Computers	n/a
Online Usage	9,591
Person/Host	18,694.61

World Wide Web Gateways

Indonesia Business Community	www.cyberdia.com
Indonesia Inc.	www.lookup.com/Homepages/71346/home.htm
Indonesian Business Center Online	www.indobiz.com

Country Domain   id

Indonesia

Indonesia ranks as one of the fastest growing, pro-business nations in South-East Asia, but it has a low score on the Global Digital Marketing Index for a number of reasons. First, Indonesia's political environment is fragile. The country has been ruled by President Suharto and the military for almost three decades. There is a growing disparity between the rich and the poor, which is being exacerbated by the expanding wealth of the upper class. Should the pro-business Suharto be replaced by an anticapitalist or fundamentalist ruler, or should the country be plunged into a working-class revolt, all foreign investments in the country will be at risk. Indonesia is also a poor digital marketing prospect because of its abysmal telecommunications infrastructure. Even in the capital of Jakarta, the telephone lines go down frequently disrupting online banking and other digital communications systems. In addition, foreign business people work under many burdensome regulations. For example, foreign businesses are not allowed to distribute their own products. They must, by law, work with native agents and distributors. And finally, the protection of intellectual property is weak; there is a thriving black market and the piracy of software is horrendous.

However, Indonesia represents a growing market of almost 200 million people. Under the auspices of Suharto, the country is desperately trying to attract foreign investment and trade. Opportunities for trade include the export to Indonesia of computers, software, scientific and laboratory equipment, medical products, and other infrastructure-related products and services.

Recommendation

For many reasons, Indonesia is not a good prospect for global digital marketing. One of these reasons is political. Many of the world's nations have condemned Indonesia's occupation of East Timor, and foreign business people from these dissenting countries have been targeted for reprisals. Another example of how politics and business don't always mix well in this complex and difficult country.

Pakistan

Index Rating	29
Position	45

Economic Environment

Purchasing Power	0.5
Economic Growth	3.5
Economic Stability	1.0
Trading Level	2.5

Population	135,000,000
Government	Federal Islamic Republic
Language	Urdu, Punjabi, English
Currency	rupee

Political Environment

Political Conditions	2.5
Freedom of Expression	3.0
Bureaucratic Index	1.0

Economic Indicators

GDP	$52,000,000,000
Per Capita	$385.19
GDP Growth	4.6%
Inflation Rate	12.3%
Exports	$9,320,000,000
Imports	$12,049,000,000

Digital & Online Environment

Telco Infrastructure	0.5
Digital Capabilities	0
Online Resources	0

Capability Indicators

Telecomm	1.3
Computers	n/a
Online Usage	511
Person/Host	264,187.87

World Wide Web Gateways

Pakistan Global Trade and Export Directory	http://globale.net/~pakistan/liste2.html
Pakistan Business Network	www.pak-economist.com
PakistanBiz.com	www.PakistanBiz.com

Country Domain   pk

Pakistan

Since its partition from India in the 1940s, Pakistan has struggled to overcome its impoverished economic conditions. During the past decade, at the urging of the International Monetary Fund (IMF), the government has made significant attempts to liberalize the economy, although these reforms have slowed in recent years. The country has suffered from ongoing political and ethnic violence, which scared away foreign investors. From a digital perspective, Pakistan is one of the developing countries that will probably leap-frog from an agricultural economy into a digital economy, bypassing the manufacturing stage experienced by most developed nations. For example, the use of cellular telephones has grown quickly in Pakistan, overcoming many of the problems stemming from its mediocre (wired) telecommunications infrastructure. However, Pakistan's digital and online capabilities are still minimal. Until online communications go wireless, the use of the Internet will be severely restricted in Pakistan, especially outside the major cities. However, the three Web sites listed here are quite good, offering organized and comprehensive access to Pakistani importers and exporters.

If you're thinking of entering Pakistan, watch out for high tariffs and other nontariff restrictions, along with a complex bureaucracy. You will also need to observe all Muslim laws governing Western-style behavior and marketing practices. For the global digital marketer, opportunities exist in the areas of telecommunications, information technology, chemicals, general machinery and equipment, food-processing equipment and technology, hydro power equipment, and transportation.

Recommendation

If Pakistan can continue to reform its economy, and expand the use of digital and online technology, the country could experience greater prosperity in the 21st century. However, at the present time, it represents only a marginal opportunity.

Russian Federation

Index Rating	29
Position	45

Economic Environment

Purchasing Power	1.0
Economic Growth	0
Economic Stability	0.5
Trading Level	1.0

Population	150,000,000
Government	Republic
Language	Russian
Currency	ruble

Political Environment

Political Conditions	1.5
Freedom of Expression	3.5
Bureaucratic Index	2.0

Economic Indicators

GDP	$793,000,000,000
Per Capita	$5,286.67
GDP Growth	-14.0 %
Inflation Rate	197.4%
Exports	$88,703,000,000
Imports	$61,147,000,000

Digital & Online Environment

Telco Infrastructure	2.0
Digital Capabilities	0.5
Online Resources	2.5

Capability Indicators

Telecomm	16.24
Computers	0.01
Online Usage	50,097
Person/Host	2,994.19

World Wide Web Gateways

Business In Russia	www.dipco.com/busrus/
Russia Business Trade Connections	www.publications-etc.com/russia/
American Chamber of Commerce in Russia	www.amcham.ru/

Country Domain   ru

Russian Federation

Since the breakup of the Soviet Union, Russia has struggled to introduce a market economy. Breaking away from a planned, centralized system has resulted in high inflation, negative growth, reduced trade, rising poverty, and increased crime and lawlessness. The populace, disenchanted by the promise of capitalist affluence, may voluntarily return to state control and oppression. The potential for this retreat is heightened by the country's lack of digital and online capabilities.

In the next decade, it is unlikely Russia will join the world élite of advanced digital economies because the country does not have the necessary conditions. The protection of intellectual property rights is nonexistent. Losses to software piracy, copyright infringements, and trademark violations run in the hundreds of millions of dollars per year. Protectionism is the norm. While tariffs on most items range from 5 to 30 percent, those imposed on luxury items can be as high as 150 percent. As well, laws governing most business practices simply do not exist.

Foreign companies operating in this environment have no legal recourse or forum in which to settle disputes. In addition, Russia does not have enough viable products or services for export. Simply put, Russia does not produce products the rest of the world would want to buy. So the future for Russia as a digital economy is bleak. The spirit of entrepreneurship has sprouted across the country, but it is unlikely that can help pull the country out of its many intractable problems. On the Web, I discovered several sites sponsored by commercial companies outside Russia.

Recommendation

For the global digital marketer interested in Russia, my advice is simple: Get paid upfront before you do business there.

Egypt

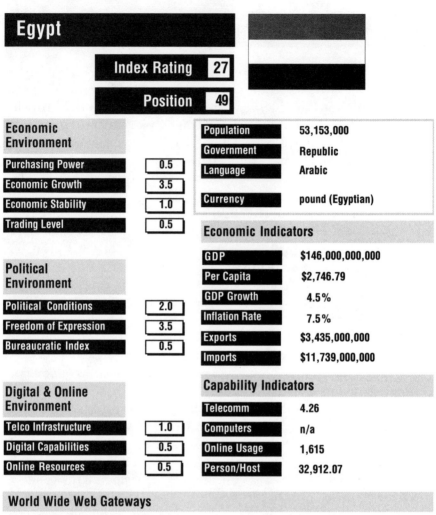

Index Rating	27
Position	49

Economic Environment

Purchasing Power	0.5
Economic Growth	3.5
Economic Stability	1.0
Trading Level	0.5

Population	53,153,000
Government	Republic
Language	Arabic
Currency	pound (Egyptian)

Political Environment

Political Conditions	2.0
Freedom of Expression	3.5
Bureaucratic Index	0.5

Economic Indicators

GDP	$146,000,000,000
Per Capita	$2,746.79
GDP Growth	4.5%
Inflation Rate	7.5%
Exports	$3,435,000,000
Imports	$11,739,000,000

Digital & Online Environment

Telco Infrastructure	1.0
Digital Capabilities	0.5
Online Resources	0.5

Capability Indicators

Telecomm	4.26
Computers	n/a
Online Usage	1,615
Person/Host	32,912.07

World Wide Web Gateways

Egypt – Global Shopping Center, Trade Zone	www.tradezone.com/shpncntr.htm
Egypt Internet Access and Information	http://pharos.bu.edu/Egypt/access.html
American Chamber of Commerce in Egypt	www.amcham.org.eg/

Country Domain   eg

Egypt

As one of the most Westernized Arab countries in the Middle East, Egypt is nonetheless a limited opportunity for the global digital marketer. The adoption of digital and online technology is hampered by the country's high level of poverty (about 15 percent of the population live close to Western standards, while the rest live in poverty), and by its outmoded telephone system. However, there are a handful of Egyptian Web sites to link you to the more sophisticated companies in Cairo. Unfortunately, trade with Egypt is also made difficult by political uncertainty, fundamentalist violence, import restrictions, red tape, and corruption.

For the bold entrepreneur, opportunities exist in Egypt for selling telecommunications equipment, electrical power supplies, aircraft parts, medical equipment, oil and gas machinery, and computer equipment. In the area of intellectual property such as software and entertainment products, be careful. Although Egypt has enacted strong intellectual property laws, enforcement has been aenemic at best. Note: In addition to the Web sites listed, another interesting place to visit is ArabNet (www. aalamalriadah.com). This site has links to all of the other countries in the Arab world.

Recommendation

With a score of only 27, Egypt has a long way to go before it becomes a digital economy. No significant opportunities here for the global digital marketing except in the area of software.

China

Index Rating	21
Position	50

Economic Environment

Purchasing Power	0.5
Economic Growth	5.0
Economic Stability	0.5
Trading Level	0.5

Political Environment

Political Conditions	1.5
Freedom of Expression	0
Bureaucratic Index	0.5

Digital & Online Environment

Telco Infrastructure	0.5
Digital Capabilities	0.5
Online Resources	1.0

Population	1,139,060,000
Government	People's Republic
Language	Mandarin
Currency	yuan

Economic Indicators

GDP	$3,000,000,000,000
Per Capita	$2,633.75
GDP Growth	11.8%
Inflation Rate	16.9%
Exports	$151,000,000,000
Imports	$139,000,000,000

Capability Indicators

Telecomm	2.29
Computers	0.01
Online Usage	68,901
Person/Host	16,531.84

World Wide Web Gateways

China Council for International Trade	www.ccpit.org
China Tenders Online	www.chinatenders.com
China Gate	www.chinagate.net

Country Domain   cn

China

As the world's most populated country, and recent acquisitor of Hong Kong, China cannot be ignored as a global digital marketing prospect. Its economy is growing rapidly, and there is an explosion of entrepreneurial activity. However, this nation of more than a billion people scored the lowest rating on the Global Digital Marketing Index. Why? It is my belief China's emergence as a significant world market will be severely constrained by its abysmal human rights record, its planned centralized economy, and most importantly, by its suppression of digital and online communications.

Although there are more than 500,000 Internet users in China, they are limited mostly to officials in the Communist Party. The average citizen does not have the capability, or the right, to freely use the World Wide Web, e-mail, and other digital tools. (See Chapter 10: The New Digital World Order.)

At the time this book was being written, China introduced sweeping laws to curtail online activity. The laws call for unspecified "criminal punishments" and fines of up to 15,000 yuan for ISPs and users who use the Web to defame government agencies or engage in other politically incorrect behavior.

Because of these repressive conditions, entering China will pose a considerable challenge to the global digital marketer. I discovered few Web sites devoted to trade which originated in China, although there are a number promoting Chinese trade which are hosted outside the country.

Recommendation

Obviously, China's huge population presents you with great potential, but it must be counter-balanced by the danger of significant risk. Its Internet policies do not bode well for the country's long-term economic prospects. I do not recommend China to anyone except the most experienced global digital marketer.

Note: The online resources for mainland China are skewed because they include the numbers for Hong Kong, where the majority of domain servers currently exist. This means the actual number of people using or having access to the Net is much lower in most regions of the country.

Economic Power

Japan	Economic Power	5.0		
GDP $5,600,000,000,000	GDP per Capita $44,800.00		Growth Rate	0.80 %

Switzerland	Economic Power	5.0		
GDP $260,000,000,000	GDP per Capita $38,736.59		Growth Rate	2.10 %

Norway	Economic Power	5.0		
GDP $135,000,000,000	GDP per Capita $31,824.61		Growth Rate	4.80 %

United States	Economic Power	5.0		
GDP $7,500,000,000,000	GDP per Capita $30,003.00		Growth Rate	2.10 %

Germany	Economic Power	5.0		
GDP $2,300,000,000,000	GDP per Capita $28,395.06		Growth Rate	2.00 %

Denmark	Economic Power	5.0		
GDP $146,000,000,000	GDP per Capita $28,076.92		Growth Rate	4.40 %

Austria	Economic Power	5.0		
GDP $202,800,000,000	GDP per Capita $26,296.68		Growth Rate	1.20 %

Finland	Economic Power	5.0		
GDP $121,000,000,000	GDP per Capita $24,267.95		Growth Rate	5.00 %

Iceland	Economic Power	5.0		
GDP $6,500,000,000	GDP per Capita $24,253.73		Growth Rate	5.20 %

Luxembourg	Economic Power	4.5		
GDP $9,200,000,000	GDP per Capita $24,146.98		Growth Rate	2.70 %

United Arab Emirates	Economic Power	4.5		
GDP $70,000,000,000	GDP per Capita $23,333.33		Growth Rate	1.70 %

Sweden	Economic Power	4.5		
GDP $196,000,000,000	GDP per Capita $22,899.87		Growth Rate	2.20 %

Belgium	Economic Power	4.5		
GDP $228,000,000,000	GDP per Capita $22,574.26		Growth Rate	2.20 %

France	Economic Power	4.5		
GDP $1,300,000,000,000	GDP per Capita $22,413.79		Growth Rate	2.20 %

Singapore	Economic Power	4.5		
GDP $66,500,000,000	GDP per Capita $22,144.52		Growth Rate	8.40 %

The Netherlands	Economic Power	4.5		
GDP $330,000,000,000	GDP per Capita $22,095.75		Growth Rate	2.50 %

Canada		Economic Power 4.0	
GDP $640,000,000,000	GDP per Capita $22,068.97	Growth Rate	4.60 %

Israel		Economic Power 3.5	
GDP $98,000,000,000	GDP per Capita $18,148.15	Growth Rate	6.70 %

United Kingdom		Economic Power 3.5	
GDP $1,024,000,000,000	GDP per Capita $17,836.30	Growth Rate	3.80 %

Italy		Economic Power 3.5	
GDP $1,010,000,000,000	GDP per Capita $17,515.87	Growth Rate	2.20 %

New Zealand		Economic Power 3.0	
GDP $53,000,000,000	GDP per Capita $15,839.81	Growth Rate	2.20 %

Ireland, Republic of		Economic Power 3.0	
GDP $53,000,000,000	GDP per Capita $15,142.86	Growth Rate	5.70 %

Australia		Economic Power 3.0	
GDP $270,000,000,000	GDP per Capita $15,000.00	Growth Rate	3.90 %

Taiwan		Economic Power 2.5	
GDP $261,000,000,000	GDP per Capita $12,857.14	Growth Rate	6.50 %

Spain		Economic Power 2.5	
GDP $483,000,000,000	GDP per Capita $12,397.65	Growth Rate	2.00 %

Malaysia		Economic Power 2.0	
GDP $193,600,000,000	GDP per Capita $9,680.00	Growth Rate	9.50 %

Greece		Economic Power 2.0	
GDP $90,000,000,000	GDP per Capita $8,890.65	Growth Rate	2.20 %

South Korea		Economic Power 2.5	
GDP $380,000,000,000	GDP per Capita $8,879.96	Growth Rate	8.40 %

Portugal		Economic Power 2.0	
GDP $90,000,000,000	GDP per Capita $8,551.07	Growth Rate	3.30 %

Saudi Arabia		Economic Power 1.5	
GDP $123,000,000,000	GDP per Capita $8,271.69	Growth Rate	2.00 %

Argentina		Economic Power 1.5	
GDP $279,000,000,000	GDP per Capita $8,205.88	Growth Rate	6.50 %

Hungary		Economic Power 1.5	
GDP $72,000,000,000	GDP per Capita $6,822.70	Growth Rate	1.00 %

Russian Federation	Economic Power	1.0		
GDP $793,000,000,000	GDP per Capita $5,286.67		Growth Rate	-14.0 %

Czech Republic	Economic Power	0.5		
GDP $49,500,000,000	GDP per Capita $4,805.83		Growth Rate	2.50 %

Mexico	Economic Power	1.0		
GDP $377,000,000,000	GDP per Capita $4,097.83		Growth Rate	4.50 %

Chile	Economic Power	1.0		
GDP $53,000,000,000	GDP per Capita $3,812.95		Growth Rate	4.20 %

Brazil	Economic Power	1.0		
GDP $550,000,000,000	GDP per Capita $3,548.39		Growth Rate	5.70 %

South Africa, Republic of	Economic Power	1.0		
GDP $122,000,000,000	GDP per Capita $3,457.85		Growth Rate	2.30 %

Turkey	Economic Power	0.5		
GDP $180,000,000,000	GDP per Capita $2,903.23		Growth Rate	-6.00 %

Venezuela	Economic Power	0.5		
GDP $56,000,000,000	GDP per Capita $2,837.60		Growth Rate	2.20 %

Egypt	Economic Power	0.5		
GDP $146,000,000,000	GDP per Capita $2,746.79		Growth Rate	4.50 %

China	Economic Power	0.5		
GDP $3,000,000,000,000	GDP per Capita $2,633.75		Growth Rate	11.80 %

Thailand	Economic Power	0.5		
GDP $143,000,000,000	GDP per Capita $2,500.17		Growth Rate	8.50 %

Poland	Economic Power	0.5		
GDP $86,000,000,000	GDP per Capita $2,252.49		Growth Rate	4.90 %

Colombia	Economic Power	1.5		
GDP $60,000,000,000	GDP per Capita $1,749.27		Growth Rate	6.50 %

Peru	Economic Power	0.5		
GDP $32,500,000,000	GDP per Capita $1,508.12		Growth Rate	7.00 %

The Philippines	Economic Power	0.5		
GDP $74,000,000,000	GDP per Capita $1,203.64		Growth Rate	5.20 %

Indonesia	Economic Power	0.5		
GDP $166,000,000,000	GDP per Capita $925.82		Growth Rate	7.30 %

Pakistan	Economic Power	0.5		
GDP $52,000,000,000	GDP per Capita $385.19		Growth Rate	4.60 %

India	Economic Power	0.5		
GDP $300,000,000,000	GDP per Capita $355.48		Growth Rate	5.00 %

Trading Level

Country			Trading Level			% of GDP
Singapore			Trading Level	5.0		
Exports	$119,000,000,000	Imports	$125,000,000,000		% of GDP	366.92
Luxembourg			Trading Level	5.0		
Exports	$6,400,000,000	Imports	$8,300,000,000		% of GDP	159.78
Ireland, Republic of			Trading Level	5.0		
Exports	$44,000,000,000	Imports	$32,000,000,000		% of GDP	143.40
Belgium			Trading Level	5.0		
Exports	$170,000,000,000	Imports	$155,000,000,000		% of GDP	142.54
The Netherlands			Trading Level	5.0		
Exports	$195,912,000,000	Imports	$176,420,000,000		% of GDP	112.83
Czech Republic			Trading Level	5.0		
Exports	$21,900,000,000	Imports	$26,600,000,000		% of GDP	97.98
Thailand			Trading Level	4.5		
Exports	$56,459,000,000	Imports	$70,776,000,000		% of GDP	88.98
Taiwan			Trading Level	4.0		
Exports	$111,585,000,000	Imports	$103,698,000,000		% of GDP	82.48
Malaysia			Trading Level	4.0		
Exports	$72,000,000,000	Imports	$72,200,000,000		% of GDP	74.48
South Korea			Trading Level	3.5		
Exports	$129,835,000,000	Imports	$150,212,000,000		% of GDP	73.70
Sweden			Trading Level	3.5		
Exports	$79,908,000,000	Imports	$64,438,000,000		% of GDP	73.65
United Arab Emirates			Trading Level	3.0		
Exports	$24,756,000,000	Imports	$19,520,000,000		% of GDP	63.25
Denmark			Trading Level	3.0		
Exports	$48,800,000,000	Imports	$43,200,000,000		% of GDP	63.01
The Philippines			Trading Level	3.0		
Exports	$17,502,000,000	Imports	$28,337,000,000		% of GDP	61.94
Portugal			Trading Level	3.0		
Exports	$22,621,000,000	Imports	$32,339,000,000		% of GDP	61.07
Poland			Trading Level	3.0		
Exports	$22,892,000,000	Imports	$29,050,000,000		% of GDP	60.40
Chile			Trading Level	3.0		
Exports	$15,000,000,000	Imports	$17,000,000,000		% of GDP	60.38

Iceland		Trading Level	2.0		
Exports	$1,898,000,000	Imports	$2,005,000,000	% of GDP	60.05

Canada		Trading Level	4.5		
Exports	$201,000,000,000	Imports	$175,000,000,000	% of GDP	58.75

Switzerland		Trading Level	3.0		
Exports	$76,196,000,000	Imports	$74,462,000,000	% of GDP	57.95

Saudi Arabia		Trading Level	3.0		
Exports	$27,829,000,000	Imports	$42,614,000,000	% of GDP	57.27

Norway		Trading Level	3.0		
Exports	$41,746,000,000	Imports	$32,702,000,000	% of GDP	55.15

New Zealand		Trading Level	3.0		
Exports	$14,442,000,000	Imports	$14,731,000,000	% of GDP	55.04

Venezuela		Trading Level	1.0		
Exports	$18,300,000,000	Imports	$11,600,000,000	% of GDP	53.39

Indonesia		Trading Level	2.5		
Exports	$45,417,000,000	Imports	$40,629,000,000	% of GDP	51.83

Israel		Trading Level	3.5		
Exports	$20,410,000,000	Imports	$29,579,000,000	% of GDP	51.01

Australia		Trading Level	2.5		
Exports	$60,000,000,000	Imports	$75,000,000,000	% of GDP	50.00

Austria		Trading Level	2.5		
Exports	$45,200,000,000	Imports	$55,300,000,000	% of GDP	49.56

United Kingdom		Trading Level	2.5		
Exports	$242,042,000,000	Imports	$263,719,000,000	% of GDP	49.39

South Africa, Republic of		Trading Level	2.5		
Exports	$29,330,000,000	Imports	$30,125,000,000	% of GDP	48.73

Peru		Trading Level	2.5		
Exports	$5,897,000,000	Imports	$9,472,000,000	% of GDP	47.29

Spain		Trading Level	2.5		
Exports	$101,999,000,000	Imports	$121,782,000,000	% of GDP	46.33

Finland		Trading Level	2.0		
Exports	$29,700,000,000	Imports	$23,200,000,000	% of GDP	43.72

France				Trading Level	2.5		
Exports	$290,000,000,000	Imports	$275,000,000,000			% of GDP	43.46
Italy				Trading Level	2.0		
Exports	$231,336,000,000	Imports	$204,062,000,000			% of GDP	43.11
Germany				Trading Level	2.0		
Exports	$521,018,000,000	Imports	$456,257,000,000			% of GDP	42.49
Pakistan				Trading Level	2.5		
Exports	$9,320,000,000	Imports	$12,049,000,000			% of GDP	41.09
Colombia				Trading Level	0.5		
Exports	$10,500,000,000	Imports	$13,700,000,000			% of GDP	40.33
Hungary				Trading Level	3.0		
Exports	$12,686,000,000	Imports	$15,896,000,000			% of GDP	39.70
Greece				Trading Level	1.5		
Exports	$9,384,000,000	Imports	$21,466,000,000			% of GDP	34.28
Turkey				Trading Level	2.0		
Exports	$21,600,000,000	Imports	$35,710,000,000			% of GDP	31.84
Mexico				Trading Level	1.5		
Exports	$48,430,000,000	Imports	$46,887,000,000			% of GDP	25.28
India				Trading Level	1.0		
Exports	$33,025,000,000	Imports	$37,177,000,000			% of GDP	23.40
United States				Trading Level	1.5		
Exports	$624,767,000,000	Imports	$817,870,000,000			% of GDP	19.24
Russian Federation				Trading Level	1.0		
Exports	$88,703,000,000	Imports	$61,147,000,000			% of GDP	18.90
Brazil				Trading Level	1.0		
Exports	$47,000,000,000	Imports	$56,000,000,000			% of GDP	18.73
Argentina				Trading Level	0		
Exports	$20,000,000,000	Imports	$20,000,000,000			% of GDP	14.34
Japan				Trading Level	1.5		
Exports	$410,929,000,000	Imports	$349,125,000,000			% of GDP	13.57
Egypt				Trading Level	0.5		
Exports	$3,435,000,000	Imports	$11,739,000,000			% of GDP	10.39
China				Trading Level	0.5		
Exports	$151,000,000,000	Imports	$139,000,000,000			% of GDP	9.67

Online Resources

Finland		Online Resources	5.0		
Domain Hosts	283,526	Population	4,986,000	Persons per Host	17.59

Iceland		Online Resources	5.0		
Domain Hosts	11,667	Population	268,000	Persons per Host	22.97

Norway		Online Resources	5.0		
Domain Hosts	171,686	Population	4,242,000	Persons per Host	24.71

United States		Online Resources	5.0		
Domain Hosts	10,000,000	Population	249,975,000	Persons per Host	25.00

Australia		Online Resources	5.0		
Domain Hosts	514,760	Population	18,000,000	Persons per Host	34.97

Sweden		Online Resources	5.0		
Domain Hosts	232,955	Population	8,559,000	Persons per Host	36.74

New Zealand		Online Resources	5.0		
Domain Hosts	84,532	Population	3,346,000	Persons per Host	39.58

Canada		Online Resources	5.0		
Domain Hosts	603,325	Population	29,000,000	Persons per Host	48.07

Denmark		Online Resources	5.0		
Domain Hosts	106,476	Population	5,200,000	Persons per Host	48.84

Switzerland		Online Resources	5.0		
Domain Hosts	129,114	Population	6,712,000	Persons per Host	51.99

The Netherlands		Online Resources	5.0		
Domain Hosts	270,521	Population	14,935,000	Persons per Host	55.21

Austria		Online Resources	5.0		
Domain Hosts	91,938	Population	7,712,000	Persons per Host	83.88

United Kingdom		Online Resources	5.0		
Domain Hosts	591,624	Population	57,411,000	Persons per Host	97.04

Luxembourg		Online Resources	5.0		
Domain Hosts	3,854	Population	381,000	Persons per Host	98.86

Singapore		Online Resources	4.5		
Domain Hosts	28,892	Population	3,003,000	Persons per Host	103.94

Germany		Online Resources	4.5		
Domain Hosts	721,847	Population	81,000,000	Persons per Host	112.21

Ireland, Republic of		Online Resources	4.5		
Domain Hosts	27,059	Population	3,500,000	Persons per Host	129.35

Israel		Online Resources	4.5		
Domain Hosts	38,494	Population	5,400,000	Persons per Host	140.28

Belgium		Online Resources	4.5		
Domain Hosts	64,607	Population	10,100,000	Persons per Host	156.33

Japan		Online Resources	4.5		
Domain Hosts	734,406	Population	125,000,000	Persons per Host	170.21

France		Online Resources	4.0		
Domain Hosts	245,501	Population	58,000,000	Persons per Host	236.25

Czech Republic		Online Resources	4.0		
Domain Hosts	41,164	Population	10,300,000	Persons per Host	250.22

Hungary		Online Resources	4.0		
Domain Hosts	29,919	Population	10,553,000	Persons per Host	352.72

Spain		Online Resources	4.0		
Domain Hosts	110,041	Population	38,959,000	Persons per Host	354.04

South Africa, Republic of		Online Resources	4.0		
Domain Hosts	99,284	Population	35,282,000	Persons per Host	355.36

Italy		Online Resources	4.0		
Domain Hosts	149,595	Population	57,662,000	Persons per Host	385.45

Portugal		Online Resources	3.5		
Domain Hosts	26,077	Population	10,525,000	Persons per Host	403.61

Taiwan		Online Resources	3.5		
Domain Hosts	34,650	Population	20,300,000	Persons per Host	585.86

Greece		Online Resources	3.5		
Domain Hosts	15,925	Population	10,123,000	Persons per Host	635.67

South Korea		Online Resources	3.5		
Domain Hosts	66,262	Population	42,793,000	Persons per Host	645.82

Poland		Online Resources	3.5		
Domain Hosts	54,455	Population	38,180,000	Persons per Host	701.13

Malaysia		Online Resources	3.5		
Domain Hosts	25,200	Population	20,000,000	Persons per Host	793.65

Chile		Online Resources	3.0		
Domain Hosts	15,885	Population	13,900,000	Persons per Host	875.04

Brazil		Online Resources	2.5		
Domain Hosts	77,148	Population	155,000,000	Persons per Host	2,009.13

United Arab Emirates		Online Resources	3.5		
Domain Hosts	1,194	Population	3,000,000	Persons per Host	2,512.56

Argentina		Online Resources	2.5		
Domain Hosts	12,688	Population	34,000,000	Persons per Host	2,679.70

Russian Federation		Online Resources	2.5		
Domain Hosts	50,097	Population	150,000,000	Persons per Host	2,994.19

Mexico		Online Resources	2.5		
Domain Hosts	29,840	Population	92,000,000	Persons per Host	3,083.11

Colombia		Online Resources	2.0		
Domain Hosts	9,054	Population	34,300,000	Persons per Host	3,788.38

Peru		Online Resources	2.0		
Domain Hosts	5,192	Population	21,550,000	Persons per Host	4,150.62

Turkey		Online Resources	2.0		
Domain Hosts	13,194	Population	62,000,000	Persons per Host	4,699.11

Thailand		Online Resources	2.0		
Domain Hosts	9,245	Population	57,196,000	Persons per Host	6,186.70

Venezuela		Online Resources	1.5		
Domain Hosts	2,417	Population	19,735,000	Persons per Host	8,165.08

China		Online Resources	1.0		
Domain Hosts	68,901	Population	1,139,060,000	Persons per Host	16,531.84

The Philippines		Online Resources	1.0		
Domain Hosts	3,628	Population	61,480,000	Persons per Host	16,945.98

Indonesia		Online Resources	1.0		
Domain Hosts	9,591	Population	179,300,000	Persons per Host	18,694.61

Egypt		Online Resources	0.5		
Domain Hosts	1,615	Population	53,153,000	Persons per Host	32,912.07

Saudi Arabia		Online Resources	0.5		
Domain Hosts	293	Population	14,870,000	Persons per Host	50,750.85

Pakistan		Online Resources	0		
Domain Hosts	511	Population	135,000,000	Persons per Host	264,187.87

India		Online Resources	0		
Domain Hosts	3,138	Population	843,931,000	Persons per Host	268,939.13

SECTION FOUR

APPENDIXES

APPENDIX A

RESOURCES

ASEAN
www.asean.or.id

ASEAN is a trading bloc consisting of Indonesia, Malaysia, Philippines, Singapore, Thailand, Brunei, Darussalam, Vietnam, and Laos. ASEAN was criticized in 1997 for admitting Myanmar due to that country's abysmal human rights record. This Web site provides access to trading opportunities within the region.

Asia Pacific Economic Cooperation
www.apecsec.org.sg

Asia-Pacific Economic Cooperation (APEC) was formed in 1989 in response to the growing interdependence among Asia-Pacific economies. Begun as an informal dialogue group with limited participation, APEC has since become the primary regional vehicle for promoting open trade and practical economic cooperation.

AT&T International Calling
www.att.com/business_traveler/

This page on the AT&T site gives you long-distance dialing information from most countries in the world.

AT&T Language Line Service
www.att.com/languageline/

Now you can communicate in almost any language over the telephone. AT&T offers a service which provides an instant translator over the telephone when you want to conduct business overseas. Check out this site for more information.

Aviation Internet Resources
http://airlines-online.com

This site provides access to more than 500 airlines and other aviation resources available on the Web.

BizTravel.com
www.biztravel.com

This site contains lots of information useful to the serious business traveler. A commercial site, but well worth a visit before venturing to another country.

Caribbean Community and Common Market NA

A trading bloc consisting of Antigua and Barbuda, The Bahamas, Barbados, Belize, Dominica, Grenada, Guyana, Jamaica, Montserrat, St. Kitts and Nevis, St. Lucia, St. Vincent and the Grenadines, Surinam, Trinidad and Tobago, and Haiti. In July of 1991, the British Virgin Islands and the Turks and Caicos Islands were granted associate membership.

CIA World Fact Book www.odci.gov/cia/publications/nsolo/wfb-all

An excellent and free resource of current information about countries. Listings are available for every country in the world.

Copyright Clearance Center www.copyright.com

Not-for-profit service which helps you protect your copyrights on the Internet.

Council of Arab Economic Unity http://mbendi.co.za/cb14.htm

The Council of Arab Economic Unity was created in order to facilitate cooperation between member Arab countries as part of a move to the creation of an Arab customs union. The council has sponsored the creation of a number of Arab joint companies and specialized trade federations which are aimed at enabling Arab companies to compete in new business sectors.

Courier Services www.fedex.com and www.ups.com

If you want to ship a package to a customer worldwide, courier companies such as FedEx and UPS ship to most major countries.

Department of Foreign Affairs www.dfait-maeci.gc.ca

This Canadian government Web site provides, among other things, travel information and advisory reports from all countries around the world.

Domain Name Registration www.internic.net

Search and register your domain name with Internic at this site.

Esprit International Corp. www.espintl.com

Calling itself "The very best Internet guide to import/export," this site contains links to international trade sites particularly useful to the import/export trader.

Global Contact Inc. www.GlobalContact.com

This Web site has been developed to offer information to help companies locate products and services worldwide. Global Contact has compiled an online directory service to assist you in locating products and services anywhere in the world. Global Contact, Inc. also supplies you with the most up-to-date news and information related to the world of international trade and transportation.

Global Digital Marketing Online
www.biginc.com

A Web site hosted by Bill Bishop's company, with current data on the Global Digital Marketing Index, plus links to all Web sites listed in this book. Also includes form for free subscription to the *Digital Marketing Report*, a monthly e-mail newsletter.

Global Internet Service Providers
thelist.internet.com

This site lists most major ISPs in countries around the world. Good start for finding an Internet connection when working off-shore.

Global Trade Center
www.tradezone.com

The Trade Zone will assist you in researching information regarding international trade. Also featured here is Global Roulette and Maps to the World. International traders can use daily the supplier bulletin board, links to suppliers' Web sites and a global chat room.

I-Trade: International Data/Trade Exchange
http://sys1.tpusa.com

Internet site listing many international trade organizations that have Web sites.

IBM Global Network Access
www.ibm.net/phoneint.html

The IBM Global Network, an Internet access service, has nearly 1,100 Internet dial access numbers in 52 countries worldwide, including over 570 in the United States and Canada. This site provides a list of the local dial-up numbers in these locations.

International Chamber of Commerce
www.iccwbo.org

The World Business Organization promotes international trade, investment, and the market economy system worldwide; makes rules that govern the conduct of business across borders; and provides services, foremost among them the ICC International Court of Arbitration, the world's leading institution of its kind.

International Monetary Fund
www.imf.org

The IMF was established in 1945 when 29 countries signed its Articles of Agreement (its Charter). The current membership is 181 countries. The purpose is to promote international monetary cooperation and to facilitate the expansion and balanced growth of international trade.

International Telephone Directory
www.infobel.be/infobel/infobelworld.html

Using this site, sponsored by Infobel, the Belgian telephone company, you can look up the telephone and e-mail address of anyone in the world. (Well, just about anyone.)

International Toll-Free Numbers
www.tollfree.att.net

Look up the international toll-free numbers of companies around the world. This is also the place to register an international toll-free number for your organization

International Trade Law Monitor
http://ananse.irv.uit.no/

A comprehensive site detailing changes to international trade laws.

LatinWorld
www.latinworld.com

LatinWorld is a directory of Internet resources for the Caribbean and Latin America.

Maritime Global Net
www.mglobal.com

This site provides information and resources for shipping your products by sea around the world.

MERCOSUR
www.mercosur.com

MERCOSUR is a trading bloc consisting of Argentina, Paraguay, Uruguay, and Brazil, representing a total population of 190 million individuals, living in an area larger than the total surface of the European continent—more than 12 million square km. In 1993, the total Gross Domestic Products (GDP) of these four nations was approximately US$715 billion.

Michigan State University
http://ciber.bus.msu.edu/busres/government

A listing of links and information on international business resources on the World Wide Web—mainly ministries of trade and/or foreign affairs for various countries.

Octagon International Business Resources
www.otginc.com

An Internet site with links to many international trade and business Web sites.

Organization for Economic Co-operation
www.oecd.org

The Organization for Economic Co-operation and Development (OECD) is an international organization with 29 member countries from North America, Europe, and the Asia-Pacific area. Collectively, OECD countries produce more than half of the world's goods and services and its members include most of the world's largest economies. The OECD is based in Paris, France, and is a forum permitting governments of the industrialized democracies to study and formulate policies regarding economic and social issues.

Rexco's International Trade Resources
www.rexco.com

This site provides links to trade-related sites in countries around the world.

TeleAdapt Online
www.teleadapt.com

If you want to know what power plugs to use in a certain country, or how to access online services while on the road, this Web site has many of the answers. A good start for the traveling global digital marketer.

The Centre for International Trade
www.centretrade.com

The Centre for International Trade (CIT) is a member organization established with the objectives to improve, facilitate, and expand international trade. The 3,500 members come from every corner of the world and include embassies, government agencies, trade associations, companies, firms and individuals.

The Economist
www.economist.com

While working on this book, I found *The Economist* to be the best source of up-to-date business information about countries around the world. I would recommend a subscription to anyone interested in global digital marketing.

The European Union
www.europa.eu.int

An economic and political unit consisting of European states including Belgium, Germany, France, Italy, Luxembourg, Netherlands (1958); Denmark, Ireland, United Kingdom (1973); Greece (1981); Spain, Portugal (1986); Austria, Finland, Sweden (1995). The EU Web site states: "The objective is to promote economic and social progress, assert the European identity on the international scene and introduce a European citizenship for the nationals of the Member States."

The NAFTA Agreement
http://the-tech.mit.edu/Bulletins/nafta.html

If you want to read over the North American Free Trade Agreement, it is all here. Good luck.

The World Bank
www.worldbank.org

The International Bank for Reconstruction and Development, frequently called the "World Bank," was established in 1944. The World Bank's goal is to reduce poverty and improve living standards by promoting sustainable growth and investments in people. The Bank provides loans, technical assistance, and policy guidance to help its developing-country members achieve this objective.

The World Trade Exchange
www.wte.net

A commercial site that provides trade news and access to worldwide trading partners.

Time Around the World
www.webcom.com/one/world/time.html

This site will tell you the time in almost every major city in the world.

Trade Compass
www.tradecompass.com

This Web site provides a host of trade-related services including an online database of global marketing leads and on-going news about international trade and commerce.

Translation Services on the Web
www.hake.com/languages.html-ssi

A complete listing of links to translation services available on the Web.

Translations
www.webcom.com/one/world/transl.html

This site will translate words or phrases in several different languages.

Travel Warnings & Advisory
http://travel.state.gov

Hosted by the U.S. State Department. Check out this site before embarking on a non-cyberspace tour of foreign countries. Fascinating.

United Nations
www.un.org

The UN Web site provides useful information about countries around the world. Worth a visit for digital marketers.

World Customs Organization
www.wcoomd.org

The World Customs Organization, established in 1952 as the Customs Co-operation Council, is an independent intergovernmental body with worldwide membership whose mission is to enhance the effectiveness and efficiency of Customs administration.

World Intellectual Property Organization
www.wipo.org

The World Intellectual Property Organization (WIPO) is an intergovernmental organization with headquarters in Geneva, Switzerland. WIPO is responsible for the promotion of the protection of intellectual property throughout the world through cooperation among states.

World Trade Centers Association
www.wtca.org

The World Trade Centers Association (WTCA) was established in 1970 to facilitate international trade by bringing together exporters and importers, and those who service these businesses. World Trade Centers are located in most major cities around the world.

World Trade Oganization
www.wto.org

The WTO is an international body dealing with the rules of trade between nations. At its heart are the WTO agreements, the legal ground-rules for international commerce and for trade policy. The agreements have three main objectives: to help trade flow as freely as possible, to achieve further liberalization gradually through negotiation, and to set up an impartial means of settling disputes.

Yahoo Exchange Rates Table
http://quote.yahoo.com/forex?update

This site, sponsored by Yahoo, provides daily quotes on major currencies. There are also two other nifty sites that do currency exchange calculations (http://www.dna.lth.se/cgi-bin/kurt/rates/) and (www.xe.net/currency/).

GLOSSARY OF TERMS

Analog: Information stored or measured as an electronic voltage is known as analog. Television, radio, VCRs, and rotary telephones use an analog method to store and transmit information.

Attractor marketing: Promotions and marketing activities designed to attract customers and prospects to a company. As opposed to proactive sales such as cold calling and direct mail.

Bandwidth: Bandwidth measures the capacity of a transmission medium such as twisted pair telephone lines, coaxial cables, or fiber-optic cables. The greater the number of bytes that can be transmitted at a time, the greater the bandwidth.

Baud rate: The rate at which digital information is transmitted and received by a modem. Baud rate is measured in bits per second (bps). Typical modems come in speeds of 14,400 (14.4 kbps) and 28,800 (28.8 kbps) bits per second. The use of cable modems promises baud rates of more than 500,000 bps.

BBS (Bulletin Board Service or System): A digital meeting place where people can exchange information over telephone lines or over the Internet. Subscribers to a BBS can post e-mail messages or digital files to online conferences, and read or download files from other subscribers. You can create your own BBS system and use it to connect your customers to your company's computer network.

Bit: A bit is a single binary digit, either 1 or 0.

Bilateral trade: Trade between two countries, usually fostered by bilateral trade agreements.

Byte: A string of eight bits (such as 10101101) is known as a byte. One thousand (1,000) bytes is equal to one kilobyte. One million (1,000,000) is equal to a megabyte.

Call centers: Telecommunications facilities used to handle incoming calls from customers and prospects around the world. Can also be used for outbound telemarketing and other telecommunications services.

Calling card: Also known as a prepaid or long-distance calling card. The holder of the card calls a 1-800 number, enters a PIN number, and makes long-distance calls based on the face value of the card (such as $5, $10, and $20). Promotional messages can be incorporated into the interactive voice-response messages heard by the caller. (Large carriers such as Bell Canada issue calling cards to their customers. These cards have a magnetic strip and a PIN number and long-distance fees are charged directly to your Bell account.)

CD-ROM: Stands for Compact Disc Read-Only Memory. It looks likes an audio compact disc and holds 640 megabytes of digital information, and is used for storing multimedia presentations and large amounts of information. To use a CD-ROM, you need a CD-ROM drive on your computer. You can produce a multimedia promotion and distribute it on CD-ROM.

Cellular radio: You can create a promotional newscast and broadcast it over the cellular telephone system. Cellular telephone users will access it by dialing a number such as *88. They will not be charged for the call. Arrangements must be made with cellular telephone companies. Costs can be offset by selling advertising to other companies.

Chat room: Many Web sites have chat rooms where you converse electronically with other Internet users. As bandwidth increases, chat rooms will incorporate live video-conferencing and virtual reality. You can set up a chat room as a promotional tool to attract people to your Web site.

Commercial online services: Large bulletin board systems that provide their own content in addition to access to the Internet. Subscribers pay a monthly fee for basic services, and a per-minute charge for specialized information. The biggest services are America Online, CompuServe, and the Microsoft Network. You can reach the subscribers of a commercial online service by sponsoring a discussion group or by setting up an online store. With the advent of the World Wide Web, the closed nature of these services calls into question their marketing potential.

Competitive digital democracy: A term coined in this book to describe the condition in which nations compete economically in the digital age through the promotion of democratic institutions and freedom of speech.

Cost-recovery marketing: Marketing activities that generate enough revenue to cover expenditures. Also known as Revenue Neutral Marketing.

Customer database: A database containing information about your customers and prospects. It can be simple, such as a mailing list, or it can be complex with extensive data on each customer.

Custom Internet platform: A private online system, developed for a specific purpose, which runs on the Internet. For example, you can create a unique ordering system for your store, which runs over the Internet. The point is, you don't need to limit yourself to the World Wide Web or other standard Internet platforms such as File Transfer Protocol (FTP). You can create your own.

Database: Like a digital filing cabinet, you use a customer database to store the names, street addresses, and telephone/fax/e-mail addresses of your customers, along with a profile of their preferences, needs, buying patterns, and credit history. A customer database is the primary digital tool of the Strategic Digital Marketing Model.

Digital: Information stored in the form of 1s and 0s is known as digital. All information stored and processed by computer, including text, sound, graphics, and video, is digital in composition. The opposite of digital is analog.

Digital assets: Assets your company has in a digital form. This includes database information, intellectual property, transactional data, multimedia content, and any other digital information which can be sold or rented to another party.

Digital checks (cheques): Digital checks contain a magnetic strip or bar code. You can issue them instead of coupons for redemption at retail stores. To redeem the digital check, the customer fills out a survey on the back and presents it to the retailer. The check is deposited by the retailer and returned to you within days through the banking system. The survey answers are scanned or manually entered into your customer database.

Digital communications audit: You conduct a digital communications audit to determine the technical capabilities and preferences of your customers and prospects. For example, you can conduct a survey to find out if your customers use the World Wide Web or if they use CD-ROMs.

Digital domain: The digital and online environment your customers and prospects enter to learn about your company and its products and services. Your Digital Domain is reached through digital tools such as the Internet, BBS, interactive voice-response, and fax-on-demand systems.

Digital infrastructure: The digital resources of a country including telecommunications, computers, and online services.

Digital intermediary: A person or organization who controls the flow of digital information for an entire industry. For example, a car dealer can set up an online service listing automobiles for sale by every car manufacturer, not just its own cars. As the digital intermediary, the dealer earns a commission on every car sold in the entire industry.

Digital marketing: The use of digital technology and processes in the development, distribution, and promotion of products and services.

Digital privacy intermediaries (DPI): Digital devices — such as anonymous e-mail, voice mail, and fax mailboxes — used to protect the personal privacy of individuals.

Digital versatile disk (DVD): A new type of CD-ROM with significantly more storage capacity than current CD-ROMs. Within a few years, you will be able to distribute elaborate multimedia promotions on DVD.

Domain name: A company address on the Internet. A typical domain name is biginc.com or biginc.on.ca. If you do not have a domain name registered, I suggest you do so immediately. If you wait, another company may take the one you want.

Electronic forms: Electronic forms are filled out on computer rather than on paper. You can send electronic order forms to your customers on disk or through e-mail. When the forms are returned to you, the data can be downloaded directly into your customer database.

E-mail: Stands for electronic mail. You can send and receive e-mail messages over the Internet or internally over private networks. Because e-mail is intrusive, it is one of the most powerful digital marketing tools.

Encryption: Methods used to secure the transmission of digital information over the Internet and over other digital media. Involves the use of complex mathematical formulas.

Encrypted data tunnel: An encrypted data tunnel secures data sent over the Internet between offices in the same company. The tunnel encrypts the data to make it unreadable to anyone who intercepts it.

Expenditure marketing: Marketing activities that are viewed as an unwelcome expense. Usually ineffective because of the lack of investment.

Fax mailbox: A fax mailbox is used to store faxes until they are retrieved by the owner of the box. To retrieve faxes, you dial a telephone number, enter a password, and indicate which fax machine you wish to have your faxes sent to. You can set up a private fax mailbox for your customers with individualized information.

Fax-on-demand: With a fax-on-demand system, you can provide customized fax information automatically upon request. To get documents, you dial up the system and enter your fax number and a code for each of the documents you desire. The documents are automatically sent within minutes to your fax machine.

Fire wall: If you have a network-wide Internet connection, you need to use a device called a fire wall to restrict access to your network from unwanted visitors on the Internet. A fire wall is essential because a network-wide connection exposes the data on your network to anyone on the Internet who has the savvy to break in.

FTP (File Transfer Protocol): You use FTP software to transfer digital files from one computer to another over the Internet.

Flatline database: A flatline database is the opposite of a relational database. Each flatline database file is a separate entity. Information cannot be shared between different database files as is the case with a relational database.

GDP (Gross Domestic Product): The total goods and services produced by a country in a given year.

GDP per Capita: The total goods and service produced by a country in a given year divided by the population. Yields an average income per person.

Global capabilities provider: A company that provides the technology facilitating global digital marketing, including call centers, Internet telephone providers, Internet Service Providers (ISP), Web server hosts, private online network hosts, prepaid calling and call-back vendors.

Global community patron: A company or individual who brings together a community of people from around the world, either in an online forum or in a traditional manner.

Global digital auctioneer: A company that hosts auctions on the World Wide Web or through a private online network.

Global digital cross-trader: A company that imports/exports goods/services in both directions between two or more countries.

Global digital entrepreneur: A company or individual who does business entirely in the digital and online realm.

Global digital exporter: A company that uses digital and online technology to export goods, services, or digital information from its own country to one or more foreign countries.

Global digital importer: A company that uses digital and online technology to import goods, services, or digital information to its own country from one or more foreign countries.

Global digital integrator: A company or individual who uses digital and online technology to bring together suppliers, employees, and customers from around the world.

Global Digital Marketing Index: A rating, provided in this book, of the 50 top digital economies in the world.

Global Digital Marketing Model: A step-by-step system for planning and implementing a global marketing program, which uses digital and online tools as its core technology.

Global digital retailer: A company that sells products or services on the Internet or through other online networks.

Global mall manager: A company that leases online space on the World Wide Web to other retailers

Global market maker: A company that runs an online trade exchange for a particular type of product, or group of products.

Global online cataloging: A Web site or other online service that features a catalog of goods, and allows for online ordering.

HTML: Stands for Hyper Text Markup Language. This is the programming language used to create content for the World Wide Web.

Ident-a-call: A digital technology used to identify the number and origin of an incoming telephone call.

Indigenous digital partners: Business relationships with agents, distributors, or representatives in a foreign country.

Industry-wide information system: An online service used to control the flow of information within an industry. The person or organization who runs an industry-wide information system is called a digital intermediary.

Interactive kiosk: An interactive kiosk is used to give customers a way to browse through information on a computer. You can set up an inexpensive interactive kiosk in your store by running an internal Web site on a stand-alone PC.

Interactive survey: A survey completed using a digital tool such as a Web site, voice-mail system, BBS, or an interactive kiosk. The results of an interactive survey are fed directly into your customer database.

Interactive television: Within a few years, your television will become a two-way digital tool that will allow you to select options using a handheld channel changer. The advent of interactive television will open up a vast new audience for digital marketers.

Interactive voice response: IVR allows you to access and select from a menu of audio information using the keys on your Touch-Tone telephone. Because everyone uses a telephone, IVR is one of the most powerful digital marketing tools.

Internet: The Internet is a global online network of computer networks.

Internet service provider (ISP): An ISP is a company that provides access to the Internet for companies and individuals.

Internet telephony: Technology that allows for low-cost, long-distance calling over the Internet. Banned in some countries.

Intranet: An internal communications system based on the World Wide Web platform. Intranets have become popular because they are easy to set up and maintain and can be accessed by many different kinds of computer platforms. Unlike the Internet, an Intranet is only accessible to people within an organization.

Investment marketing: Marketing projects viewed as an investment, rather than as a cost.

IP address: An IP Address is your numeric address on the Internet (i.e., 121.154.6.44.).

Latent digital capabilities: Digital capabilities and information resources in your organization not being utilized to their fullest potential.

Loyalty card programs: Programs set up by a company to reward its best customers and to encourage repeat business. Members of a loyalty program usually receive points or other rewards by presenting a plastic card when making a purchase.

Mail list server: Used to distribute e-mail messages to a group of people on the Internet. To join a mailing list about a particular subject (e.g., bonsai tree pruning), you send an e-mail message to the mail list server. You can set up an Internet mailing list to send out information to your customers and prospects.

Market segment: A market segment is a part of your total market defined by particular common characteristics.

Market segmentation: The division of customers and prospects into smaller, well-defined groups.

Marketing myopia: A term coined by Theodore Levitt to describe the condition in which a company loses sight of its real business or mandate. For example, a bank isn't only in the banking business; it's in the financial services business.

Marketing technopia: A term I coined to describe the condition in which a company becomes obsessed with technology and forgets its customers and its real business objectives.

Modem: Stands for modulator/demodular. A device used to send and receive digital information from one computer to another over telephone lines.

Multi-lateral trade: The exchange of goods and services between three or more countries. Usually facilitated by multilateral trade agreements.

Multimedia: Refers to the use of text, graphics, audio, and video to present digital information.

Network-wide Internet connection: Also known as a full Internet connection, it means a network of computers connected continuously to the Internet over high-speed data lines.

Newsgroups: Discussion groups on the Internet, which cover a particular subject. There were more than 20,000 newsgroups on the Internet as of September 1996.

Niche-to-niche marketing: The marketing of a specialized product or service to a specialized group of customers and prospects.

Online services: Information and function-related services accessed using a modem and a computer. The Internet, BBSs, and commercial services, such as America Online and CompuServe, are examples of online services.

Online shopping: The purchase of products and services using online services such as the World Wide Web.

Online shopping malls: World Wide Web sites featuring a number of different stores offering a wide range of products and services.

Pay phone services: A service that pays people to listen to promotional messages over the telephone, similar to a reverse 1-900 number.

Personal digital assistant (PDA): Small handheld computers that allow you to send and receive e-mail and fax messages over wireless or cellular transmission systems.

Personal identification number (PIN): A series of numbers or letters to identify a person as the rightful owner of a transaction medium such as a banking or smart card.

Private online network: An online network that can be accessed only by people who have a user ID and a password. As a marketing tool, you can set up a private online network for your customers. It is also known as a BBS.

Privacy agent: In the near future, privacy agents will be used to protect the privacy of individuals. If a marketer wants information about a person, he or she will approach the privacy agent and negotiate a price for data.

Privacy ombudsman: An individual appointed in a company or organization to champion the privacy rights of customers. For example, a privacy ombudsman makes sure customer data is not used in an unethical manner.

PUSH technology: A online technology that transmits multimedia information over the Internet to a subscriber's personal computer.

RAM (random access memory): The live, active memory of your computer measured in megabytes. Most new computers run on at least 6 megabytes of RAM.

Relational database: This is a database format which allows information in different database files to be shared with each other. When you set up a customer database, use a relational database program.

Revenue Marketing: Marketing activities that generate more revenue than the cost of producing them.

Request for Proposal (RFP) robots: Future devices and processes that will allow you to make your consumer needs known to marketers while maintaining your anonymity.

Search engine: Search engines are used on the Internet to find Web sites. They are also used to find information in a database.

Smart cards: Cards that can receive, store, and transmit digital information such as electronic money or medical records.

Strategic Digital Marketing Model: A model I created to guide you in the development of marketing programs using digital and online technology.

TCP/IP (transmission control protocol/Internet protocol): All information transmitted over the Internet must be formatted based on the TCP/IP standard. You can create your own Internet platform as long as it adheres to TCP/IP.

Universal Resource Locator (URL): This is the address of your Web site on the Internet. A typical URL is http://www.biginc.on.ca

Value-Added Processor: A company or individual who adds value to a product or service at some point in the manufacturing or delivery process.

Video-mail: The next generation of e-mail. Digital video images are captured using a digital camera and sent as an attachment to an e-mail message. The recipient can open the message and view the video. It won't become practical until greater bandwidth is available.

Virtual Reality (VR): The use of sophisticated hardware and software to simulate a "virtual" environment. Although the commercial applications of VR are limited and expensive at this time, it will become more viable as computers become more powerful in the next 10 years.

Web server: The computer that holds your Home Page and other documents on the World Wide Web. It is connected directly to the Internet and is accessed using a browser software such as Netscape Navigator or Mosaic.

Web site: Your content on the World Wide Web. A Web site is located on a computer connected directly to the Internet.

World Wide Web: The most commercial platform on the Internet, which allows users to jump from one computer to another on the Internet to view pages with text, graphics, and other multimedia features.

APPENDIX C

SUGGESTED READING

Arnold, David. *The Age of Discovery*. New York: Methuen, 1983.

Barber, Benjamin R. *Jihad vs. McWorld*. New York: Ballantine Books, 1995.

Boorstin, Daniel J. *The Discoverers*. New York: Random House, 1983.

Boss, George F. *A History of Seafaring*. New York: Walker & Company, 1972.

Czinkota, Michael R., and Ilkka A. Ronkainen. *International Marketing*. Orlando: The Dryden Press, 1990.

Downs, Robert Bingham. *In Search of New Horizons: Epic Tales of Travel and Exploration*. Chicago: American Library Association, 1978.

Holmes, Kim, Bryan Johnson, and Melanie Kirkpatrick. *1997 Index of Economic Freedom*. Washington, D.C.: The Heritage Foundation, 1997.

Homer (translated by E.V. Rieu). *The Odyssey*. London: Penguin Books, 1991.

Hyde, Walter Wodburn. *Ancient Greek Mariners*. Oxford: Oxford University Press, 1947.

Kidron, Michael, and Ronald Segal. *The State of the World Atlas*. London: Penguin Books, 1995.

Leaptrott, Nan. *Rules of the Game: Global Business Protocol*. Cincinnati, OH: Thomson Executive Press, 1996.

Morrison, Terri, Wayne A. Conaway, and Joseph J. Douress. *Doing Business Around the World*. Englewood Cliffs, NJ: Prentice Hall, 1997.

Nowell, Charles E. *The Great Discoveries.* Cambridge: Cambridge University Press, 1997.

Owen, Roderic. *Great Explorers.* New York: Mayflower Books, 1979.

Penrose, Boise. *Travel and Discovery in the Renaissance.* Cambridge, MA: Harvard University Press, 1967.

Randier, Jean. *Men and Ships Around Cape Horn.* New York: David McKay Company, 1966.

Rugman, Alan M., and Richard M. Hodgetts. *International Business: A Strategic Management Approach.* New York: McGraw-Hill, 1995.

Throwler, Norman J.W. *Sir Francis Drake and the Famous Voyage 1577-1580.* Los Angeles: Center for Medieval and Renaissance Studies, 1984.

Thurmond, Molly E. *World Trade Almanac.* San Rafael, CA: World Trade Press, 1996.

Wilcox, Desmond. *Ten Who Dared.* Boston: Little, Brown and Company, 1977.